HOW ORDINARY PEOPLE
CAN BECOME
EXTRAORDINARY LEADERS

HOW ORDINARY PEOPLE CAN BECOME EXTRAORDINARY LEADERS

Empowerment Principles for Leadership Success

By

Dr. Don Panhorst

Baton Publishing Company
P.O. Box 725
Edinboro, PA 16412-0725

LCCN 92-75737

ISBN 0-9634723-4-8

Editing, design, typesetting, and printing services provided by About Books, Inc., 425 Cedar Street, Buena Vista, CO 81211, 800-548-1876.

ATTENTION: CORPORATIONS, GOVERNMENT AGENCIES, PROFESSIONAL ORGANIZATIONS, AND EDUCATIONAL INSTITUTIONS: Quantity discounts are available on bulk purchases of this book for educational purposes, gifts, or fund raising. Special books or book excerpts can also be created to fit specific needs. For information, please contact Baton Publishing Company, P.O. Box 725, Edinboro, PA 16412-0725.

Dedication

Dedicated to my loving wife, companion and friend, Dorothy, and our children Lynda and David.

Table of Contents

Introduction

"There is in most Americans some spark of idealism, which can be fanned into a flame. It takes sometimes a divining rod to find what it is; but when found, and that means often, when disclosed to the owners, the results are often extraordinary."

—*Justice Louis Dembitz Brandeis* [1]

---

[1] Louis Brandeis, *The Words of Justice Brandeis*, ed. Solomon Goldman, (New York: Henry Schuman 1953), p. 30.

The Element of the Extraordinary

I have a profound vision for the leaders of tomorrow, and it doesn't hinge on people like the President of the United States, General H. Norman Schwarzkopf or even Lee Iacocca. It involves you and me, your neighbor down the street and the little old man who runs the newspaper stand on the corner.

For years leadership has been missing one of its most vital ingredients—the element of the extraordinary. I'm convinced that in the past we've been misled to believe that element came from superstar leaders whose great works were splashed across the headlines.

The truth is it doesn't.

Instead, the extraordinary comes from the quiet corners of ordinary lives. It comes from the lives of people like those you will read about in this book: the selflessness of a young boy in East St. Louis, the determination of a firefighter in Canada and the concern of an old man who liked to write letters.

It's time we realized the era of "bigger-than-life" leaders is over. Superstar leadership is quickly fading into the past.

The Leadership Vacuum

There's no doubt about it. Our nation is crying out for insightful, influential leaders in the top management positions of institutions, businesses and governmental bodies. In this age of technology, competition and fast-paced, high-energy living, our world is obsessed with microchips, microwaves, instant coffee and instant gratification.

3

Society's focus is so technology-oriented, it has unconsciously stripped itself of the most vital ingredient needed for shaping its future—effective leaders.

We've discovered over the past few decades that we live in a huge leadership vacuum. Where have all our truly great leaders gone? We've stood open-mouthed as those who claimed to have the "right stuff" to effectively lead our governments, businesses, schools, churches and organizations have allowed themselves to be dragged into a quagmire of greed, timidity, empty rhetoric, questionable practices and incompetency.

Ruthlessly consuming its victims, the leadership vacuum has spared no one. It has sucked up everyone from the President of the United States to the messengers of the Gospel.

In the past, to resolve our leadership dilemma we've concentrated on improving the top leaders of our organizations. But that approach has repeatedly failed. Our environment has changed too much for top-down leadership to be effective. We're in an age of decentralization. Businesses have discovered it is easier to run their companies without the old hierarchical structure, and more and more people are leading small groups within large organizations.

The business climate is shifting. Specialized businesses will soon be the only ones surviving. Downsizing has eliminated many middle managers. In addition, volunteerism is rapidly becoming an economic necessity. The pressures of time, money and competition are forcing us to increasingly rely on individual empowerment.

The Birth of a New Kind of Leadership

The good news is: The vacuum has not consumed *all* of our leadership potential. It has yet to swallow you and me. If we stand up and do something about it now, the vacuum will not have a chance to consume us.

I believe the power behind our leadership lies with the average person. People like you and I *can* make a difference—whether it be in our homes, schools, communities, jobs, churches or clubs. You and I can contribute, no matter how insignificantly, to society. We can inspire others to do the same.

I wrote *How Ordinary People Can Become Extraordinary Leaders* because I believe by sharing my vision with you, we can do something *today* to start making an impact in our world. I will admit it's not an easy task, but it is achievable.

Even though many of us have long had the desire to lead, we don't quite know how to go about it. For instance, we don't know how to motivate others to our cause. We've wondered where to find people who were willing to commit themselves to embarking on inspired visions.

We're afraid to take the risks involved, to venture forth in leadership roles; worse yet, we're afraid of failing. And we don't like the idea of striking out alone without some form of guidance.

Now we can push all of that fear and intimidation aside. We don't have to accept the fact that we're *just* ordinary people—we're ordinary people with the *potential* for extraordinary accomplishments.

I believe the key to leadership is, as Dwight David Eisenhower put it, "the art of getting someone else to do something that you want done because he wants to do it." In other words, it is grassroots leadership. And this kind of leadership is not just becoming more popular, it's becoming *essential* for all types of institutions.

What This Book Offers You

By picking up this book you've taken the first step to discovering your potential. You've opened the opportunity to:

- Shatter the leadership illusion and understand why people at the bottom of the spectrum really have the most control.

- Learn how you can draw out extraordinary abilities from your ordinary life.

5

- Discover how you can experience personal satisfaction from leading in relatively narrow spheres of influence, whether with your child's little league team, the local rotary club, the Red Cross chapter, or a departmental core group at the office.

- Read stories about everyday people, from school children to senior citizens, who have grown personally through their efforts and have made a remarkable difference in our nation's broad leadership perspective.

If you're the type of person who's anxious to become a leader, then my vision is your vision. You *can* uncover the secret to empowering yourself to extraordinary leadership. I've created a strategy for helping you do just that by focusing on the transformational process of *experiencing* the leadership role.

In other words, any book can inform you *what* to do, *how* to do it and *when* to do it. But no book in the world can unveil *why* to do it the way experience can. I believe experience is our key to understanding. That's what makes this book so unique.

How Ordinary People Can Become Extraordinary Leaders is a compilation of years of experience. It's not built around the superstar success stories business leaders and politicians often collect, although it does utilize some such illustrations. Instead, it's an exploration of the kind of ordinary, often unimpressive leadership roles most people are faced with. More importantly, it's an assessment of the empowerment principles that can make you the kind of leader who impacts our world.

I've spent nearly 40 years involved in some type of leadership role. My lifetime leadership abilities were spawned in the band room at a school in Saint Clair, Missouri. They eventually extended to naval units, universities, community groups and professional organizations.

Since those early days, I've earned a Doctor of Musical Arts degree and gained extensive experience as a musician and conductor. I've spent more than 32 years in the education field, mastering my skills as a teacher, professor, administrator,

6

academic dean and vice president; I've served 23 years in the U.S. Naval Reserve, retiring as a commander, and volunteered on numerous boards of professional and civic organizations.

My career has taken me through nearly every leadership realm that exists. It's not a glorious career. As a matter of fact, it's pretty ordinary. What's important is the knowledge that I can make a difference.

In this book, I hope to encourage you to discover that same reality through some of my personal stories and those of others who have made an impact through their daily leadership roles. As you read each chapter you will gain an understanding of the 10 empowerment principles necessary for transforming yourself into an extraordinary leader.

You and I both know it's time for the emergence of a new breed of leader—not just someone who might be seated in the Oval Office or in an 11th-story penthouse. So, be bold. Recognize that new breed of leader is *you*.

1

The Leadership Challenge

"As orchestra conductors say, it is important to build up the oboist as an oboist, but it is even more important to build up the oboist's pride in the performance of the orchestra. You can reconcile the two, but it puts a tremendous premium on having very clear goals and a very clear and demanding mission for the enterprise."

—Peter Drucker [2]

---

[2] Peter Drucker, "Managing The Post-Business Society," *Fortune,* July 3, 1989, p. 70.

Experiencing the Vision

With great anticipation you're awaiting the beginning of the performance, but you cringe at the seeming disorderliness of the pre-concert ritual. One hundred people sit on stage, each appearing lost in his or her own thoughts. All that reaches your ears is the chaotic noise of more than 20 different kinds of instruments clamoring to get in tune.

A cellist quickly rosins her bow, dusts off the neck of her instrument and saws the bow across the strings to check them. The percussionist repositions the kettledrums and chimes, then gives the tympanums a roll to assure they're in tune. You wonder how this unorganized group can be a world-class orchestra that performs beautiful music.

Finally the house lights dim as the concertmaster stands before the ensemble. Suddenly the atmosphere changes as all instrumentalists quietly match their pitches to that of the oboe. Then, deathly silence falls across the concert hall. As the conductor walks briskly to the platform, the clicking of his sparkling, black patent leather shoes echoes through the hall. The audience explodes with applause. He bows deeply, turns and steps onto the podium. He looks out over the orchestra and the musicians quickly sit up straight, position their instruments and fix their gaze intently on his baton. Slowly the conductor's arms rise and, once again, a hush falls across the hall. At last, the baton falls.

The tympani rumble a deep, ominous tone. The cellos and basses softly tremolo, then slowly increase in intensity as they crescendo into a powerful surge of expectation. The cymbals

11

crash. The trumpets flourish. The strings pierce the air with quick, forceful strokes. You sit spellbound as a hundred individual musicians mysteriously meld into one gigantic organism—the New York Philharmonic Orchestra in all its glory.

You've forgotten the awful sawing, bleating, bumping noises you heard moments earlier. The concert hall reverberates as a Beethoven masterpiece comes alive and dances across the strings of violins and violas and leaps from the woodwind and brass sections. The production seems almost effortless. Yet you're captured by its energy. You feel a magnetism. You know you're hearing true music.

What you may not know is you're also seeing the birth of a truly inspired vision. You're experiencing true leadership.

The Music Behind the Music

The truth is, when it comes to leadership, most of us have been sadly disillusioned. For so long we've had a distorted image of what we call the "Great Leader." It's time we put a stop to blindly accepting the old leadership paradigm and gain an understanding of exactly what leadership is. I just shared with you my image of true leadership by helping you visualize an orchestra concert.

Most of us recognize that the ability to perform concerts doesn't come suddenly or easily. It takes hard work, dedication and leadership. Many people would also agree that the conductors are the leaders in this type of situation, but I believe they're only a small part of the leadership picture. Grassroots leadership, the kind of leadership this country needs now more than ever, is present not just in the conductor, but in each individual musician.

Since my career has revolved around music as a saxophonist and conductor, I've experienced grassroots leadership firsthand. I believe it resembles music more closely than anything else I know. They're both art forms.

When I refer to grassroots leadership, I'm talking about the foundation upon which our country was created. It's the kind of

12

leadership that begins with ordinary people, like you and me, who want to accomplish extraordinary things.

When I think back on most of those who we consider the great musicians of all time, I can't help but notice they started out as plain, ordinary people. None were really born the superstars they became. For instance, few had heard of Johann Sebastian Bach until he replaced an elderly church organist.

One evening in a cathedral the old musician gave Bach the key to the organ, and when the young man sat down at the bench, he played with such genius, the aging organist's eyes filled with tears. This was the world's first exposure to Bach, and it wasn't in a magnificent concert hall with standing-room only. It was in an ordinary church on an ordinary night in front of a rather ordinary musician.

Becoming the kind of master at music that Bach was certainly didn't happen overnight, and becoming a master at leadership won't happen that way either. The members of the New York Philharmonic have dedicated much of their lives to practicing and mastering their art. The same must be true for people wishing to master leadership.

So What Is Grassroots Leadership?

Summed up in one sentence, *effective leadership is the harmonious rendition of an inspired vision.* In other words, the product of effective leadership is the successful delivery of a high quality result. If you remember in the orchestra concert mentioned earlier, the New York Philharmonic performed a marvelous example of effective leadership. They produced an extraordinary delivery of Beethoven's score. Whether your leadership role involves raising money for the Red Cross, coaching your child's little league team or teaching a Sunday school class, your success *depends* upon the delivery of a high quality result.

Let's look a little more closely at that definition of effective leadership. An inspired vision is a dream of greatness—not of personal greatness, but of great *results*. Effective leadership is inspired because it's our own expression of something worth

13

pursuing, and it's a vision because it reflects with amazing clarity how we interpret the world.

Imagine yourself as a composer for a moment. You're not just trying to write music; you're trying to create your vision. Like composers we each have an overall picture of what we want to accomplish in life, what kind of impact we want to leave in the world. That vision may not be clear to all of us, but it's there. Remember, Beethoven was deaf in his later years, yet he could envision how he wanted his music to affect people, what kind of reaction it would evoke, and what kind of satisfaction it would provide him.

Some composers, like Beethoven, can imagine in their mind's ear the structure and combination of melodies, harmonies and the orchestration they wish to use in a composition. The composer then creates in his mind a finished piece of music which can be transferred to paper. This is truly inspired vision.

Now a harmonious rendition is the combined effort that allows your inspired vision to become reality. For example, when an orchestra plays a piece by Beethoven, it attempts—through the conductor and each musician—to accurately achieve the result the composer envisioned. The musicians work as a team so they can successfully deliver his music to the audience the way they think Beethoven would have wanted it.

In a fine orchestra, each musician assumes personal responsibility for performing his or her part. The leader of each instrumental section provides guidance which the section members follow in executing the phrasing and special nuances called for in the music. The conductor, then, unifies and inspires the musicians to re-create the musical composition to conform to his or her interpretation of the score. The result is a harmonious rendition of a musical masterpiece.

For you and me, the task is much the same. We must constantly strive to achieve a harmonious rendition of our vision, not through our efforts alone, but through the efforts of the entire group we lead. The result must be harmonious—unified. And it must be a rendition—a translation of the vision.

14

Leadership ability, like musical prowess, is a highly complex art form requiring great dedication and practice. Its complexity is not so much in technicality as it is in lifestyle. Leadership is a way of life. That's why it's possible for ordinary people to become the composers, conductors and musicians of extraordinary masterpieces.

If This Is the Way It's Supposed To Be, Then Where Are All Our Leaders?

If leadership is supposed to work like a finely conducted orchestra, then why aren't we hearing more beautiful music? Where have all our leaders gone? Why do we have such a hard time pinpointing the great leaders of our time? Remember, we're suffering from a leadership vacuum. Author and leadership consultant, Warren Bennis has said:

> "At the heart of America is a vacuum into which self-anointed saviors have rushed. They pretend to be leaders, and we—half out of envy, half out of longing—pretend to think of them as leaders . . . Some say that leaders are born, while others argue that they can be made, and—according to the one-minute manager and/or microwave theory—made instantly. Pop in Mr. and Ms. Average and out pops another McLeader in sixty seconds." [3]

We've created an illusion of leadership, ascribing bigger-than-life qualities to individuals. Unfortunately, because we've pretended for so long that this is what makes true leaders, many of our "saviors" have fallen from grace.

We've watched our so-called superheroes admit to, or at least get caught in, deceit, moral failure, illegalities, greed and fraud. In the Iran-contra scandal some of our most honored military and political leaders deceived Congress and the American nation

---

[3] Warren Bennis, *Why Leaders Can't Lead* (San Francisco: Jossey-Bass Publishers, 1989), p. 36-37.

to hide their involvement in channeling illegal funds to aid the Nicaraguan contras.

On the business scene, we've suffered from the lack of effective leadership as developing countries continue to beat us to the punch in the global market. For the first time in more than two centuries, the United States must play "catch up" to foreign competitors.

In our churches we've witnessed a wave of pseudoleaders. Christians and non-Christians alike stood aghast as evangelists Jim Bakker and Jimmy Swaggert both admitted to participating in extramarital sexual trysts—behaviors they so vehemently preached against.

Even our cities have been affected by this leadership illusion. Washington, D.C., the capital of our country, became a national disgrace mainly because of the corruption of its mayor, Marion Barry. His mayoral terms were strewn with scandals of numerous sexual liaisons, undocumented traveling expenses, allegations of cocaine use and finally an arrest and indictment for possession and use of crack.

Don't get me wrong, I'm not suggesting for one minute that our country is void of good leadership. What I am saying is it's just not as easy as some of our well-known leaders have persuaded us to believe. There's more to leading cities and countries than finesse and personality. We can't just go to a drive-thru and pick up all that's necessary to become Joe McLeader. The problems that are unique to our era make it much more difficult than that.

Why Is It So Hard to Lead People Today?

Never before have we lived in such a self-focused society. Never before have we had the choice of so many accessible options. And never before have we had to live with the kind of work ethic that places almost all the emphasis on the wants and needs of the individual. Let's look at some of the reasons leadership is so hard today.

16

A. ***It's becoming increasingly difficult to get people to participate or cooperate in any type of combined effort.***

Have you tried recently to organize a group of people for a common cause? Maybe you wanted to set up a fund-raiser at church, get volunteers for the local YMCA picnic or put together a presentation for work. For some reason you couldn't get people to commit themselves to the task. Why not? What is it that causes people to shy away from commitment? I've found there are two main reasons:

Lack of time

Even though we live in an instant society that's supposed to help us shave off minutes traveling, cleaning, cooking and doing thousands of other things, we still complain about not having enough time in our days. We're constantly pressed with balancing our professional and personal lives.

People want the best of both worlds. They want challenging careers, yet quality time with their families and social circles. After working eight-hour days (often much more), taking the kids to athletic or music practice, attending parent-teacher meetings and finishing household chores, who has the time or the desire to commit to a fund-raising project?

Too many distractions and varied interests

Distractions are inevitable. They have to get a project finished at work. They have to throw a birthday party for their daughter. They have to plan the Rotary Club dinner.

It's no wonder our minds are often too occupied to concentrate on one particular item. Our lives are overflowing with distractions.

Today, so many activities are available to choose from that it allows people to have varied interests. They no longer have to be content with just belonging to the church fellowship or the lodge. Now people can choose from thousands of advocacy and self-help groups, hundreds of clubs and civic organizations. And they're more

17

apt to decline participating in your project when their social life revolves around another organization they feel is more important.

B. *A general lack of commitment is prevalent in most organizations.*

It's an indisputable fact that most people are not committed to their organizations as much as they're committed to themselves. Even though the new work ethic reveals that people want to be more involved, the main reason they do is selfish.

The truth is when it comes to combined efforts, organizations can't get full commitments from their people. Teachers can't get students to sign up for the drama club. Companies can't get people to attend board meetings, and churches can't get people to take turns attending the nursery.

Many people have allowed their individual concerns to overshadow public good. Instead of being committed to visions of common good—like finding cures for terminal diseases, discovering ways to make more use of solar energy or creating plans for saving our environment—people are committed to matters of self-interest.

Far too many people just aren't as interested as they used to be in new, fresh ideas; they don't care about becoming more competitive in the international market, raising money for a combination soup kitchen and shelter or stopping injustice. They want quick-fixes and easy answers.

We, as a culture, seem to have lost sight of the glorious things we can do when we work together. We don't seem to have a vision of what we can become as a nation, as organizations, as communities or even as families. We're more noncommittal than ever because we're smothered by short-term thinking and lack of vision.

18

C. ***People fear becoming victims of leadership paralysis.***
Some people secretly suffer from leadership paralysis; they're gripped by fear.

They fear failure
I only know a few people in the world who aren't afraid of failure, but people who suffer from leadership paralysis have an unhealthy fear. They don't just fear making mistakes or missing a deadline; they fear *potential* failure, and steer away from anything that remotely resembles it.

They insulate themselves from risk, criticism and rejection
Many people live in self-imposed safety nets. To them, leadership represents the unknown and anything unknown is risky. Leadership roles can mean danger, possible instability and a loss of control. And many people have to insulate themselves from that kind of risk. To avoid what they consider danger zones, they let someone else map out the way.

They don't know how to handle the newly restructured organizational environment
In an age where "downsizing" and "flattening the pyramid" are buzzwords, it's not unusual for people to fear the new business structure. Since the leadership hierarchy in traditional business has become almost horizontal, more and more people are realizing they must hone their skills. And for many people, this new environment is frightening.

The Good News Is . . . You Can Do It!

The leadership vacuum has discouraged many potential leaders. But don't let that affect you! Our country needs people like you and me to stand up and make a difference. The fact that you're reading this book proves you're willing to take the first step forward.

If you really want to become an effective leader, let me mention a few things. Extraordinary leadership is an exciting vision, but it does require you to make some changes in your life. You must be willing to walk down the road to a new frontier. You need to discover what true leadership is and discard all the old definitions you've learned. You have to become a pioneer.

You must also be willing to pay the price. Change doesn't come without sacrifice, and success doesn't come free of charge. You must dedicate your time and energy to transforming yourself into an extraordinary leader.

The Paradigm Is Dead . . . But Leadership Isn't

Unfortunately, we can't embark on a mission to create extra-ordinary leaders by examining the past. We've experienced an onslaught of pseudoleaders and, sadly, we no longer have role models to seek guidance from. In the past, we looked to kings, generals and industry moguls. But the paradigm they fit into has long been dead. The era of the superhero is gone.

For years we allowed ourselves to believe an ideal that discolored the image of an effective leader. Our society tried to create a simple, cut-and-sew pattern for leadership. The people who knew how to say the right things, make the right moves, maintain their popularity and still keep their charismatic flair were the ones who fit the part.

In this self-imposed mold or paradigm, we were led to believe that people gained their leadership savvy through one of three ways:

1. They were blessed with innate abilities.

2. They had an uncanny talent for beating the odds and using their circumstances to get them to the top.

3. Or, they were just plain lucky.

Regardless of how a person achieved leadership skill, in this paradigm *only* those who achieved superstar status were considered true leaders. So if this whole paradigm is all a hoax, why have we believed it for so long?

20

Unfortunately, the hierarchical structure of most organizations entrapped us into believing it. Leadership positions have often been identified by the long climb to the top of the organizational pyramid. And once there, people revelled in gaining ultimate power and prestige.

People within organizations coveted a place on the executive fast-track for "deliverance" to the top of the "mount." However, only because many of our leaders have been getting caught in scandal have we finally realized the fallen heros aren't really the "saviors" we once thought they were.

The truth is: Leadership is neither a gift acquired by birth, chance or special powers nor a process of mastering control over time, money or people. In the past few decades, people who have tried to lead either with an iron fist or with their innate prowess haven't survived very long in our society.

For you and me the vision is clear; we must abandon the old paradigmatic approach to leadership. We can no longer glorify leadership positions. We cannot envy the roles as if they would fill us with god-like qualities or assume that leadership positions give us the authority to be dictators.

Instead, we must capture the vision of grassroots leadership—being personally responsible for seeing changes in our world and filling the leadership vacuum.

The Leadership Shift

Fortunately, some people are becoming personally responsible for changing the world. Something new is emerging, and they're finally starting to fight back against old leadership practices. For instance, in countries all over the world, people are clamoring for freedom to participate in their governments and to make a difference.

Most recently we've seen an increase in riots, coups and protests in an effort to eliminate oppression. In Beijing, China, we watched tens of thousands of Chinese students ban together in Tiananmen Square to demand freedom from the Communist regime. They erected a scaled-down version of the Statue of Liberty, and carried out their vigil for more than three weeks before the government ordered the military to begin "disbanding" the protesters. In the absence of quality leadership, the regime had to rely on brute force to avert total chaos.

People in Eastern bloc countries have broken from under the rigidity of their countries' rule. We've seen oppressive pseudo-leaders topple like dominoes. Germany opened up the wall between the East and West. Poland and Czechoslovakia removed their Communist governments, Romania executed its dictatorial leaders, and the Soviet Union no longer exists.

In South Africa protestors continue to struggle to eliminate apartheid in the predominantly black nation. Progress is slow but evident. Nelson Mandela was freed after 27 years of imprisonment, and negotiations were begun between the black and white political leaders.

Ordinary people everywhere are struggling to put effective leaders at the reins. Students, factory workers and housewives are wanting to influence decisions, and it's time we started letting them do so.

Transforming Individuals

My goal for this book is to teach ordinary people how to achieve high quality results through their leadership abilities—to be at the same time, composers of a vision and musicians of a product. In other words, I want to show *you* how to get people to translate your vision because they want to do it. And the only way to achieve that is for us to change the way we view leadership.

First, we need to realize that leaders are not born; they're made through *education*. People cannot become leaders just by incorporating 20 tips into their leadership style, altering their environments to facilitate effectiveness or copying the methods of those who have travelled the road to success before them. That's *schooling*, not education.

Second, no amount of *external* change is going to make a significant difference in one's leadership approach. People will only see results when they understand there must be an *internal* change. Leaders can't talk right and walk left; that just proves that external change does nothing for a person's credibility. Leadership involves transforming individuals into leading new lifestyles.

This internal transformation doesn't happen overnight. It's often a slow and painful process because it involves changing our habits and altering our way of life. Niccolo Machiavelli once quite accurately described the difficulty in change:

> *"It must be considered that there is nothing more difficult to carry out, nor more doubtful of success, nor more dangerous to handle, than to initiate a new order of things. For the reformer has enemies in all those who would profit by the old order, and only lukewarm defenders in all those who would profit by the new order, this lukewarmness arising partly from fear of their adversaries, who have the laws in their favour; and partly from the incredulity of mankind, who do not truly believe in anything new until they have had actual experience of it."* [4]

Becoming a great leader is truly like playing in an orchestra. The way one violinist performs has an affect on how the entire violin section plays. Therefore, that section's presentation affects how the entire orchestra performs. Leadership starts with one person perfecting his or her role as an individual. It involves the leader's conscious efforts to work toward the good of the whole.

Remember, individual musicians who play in orchestras master their performances for the good of the entire ensemble, not just for their personal satisfaction. Each musician knows his or her part is needed for the music to be properly executed, but each also knows that without the rest of the orchestra his or her part loses most of its impact.

For leaders, this same analogy holds true. Harry J. Gary, chairman of United Technologies Corporation, once said, "How

---

[4] Niccolo Machiavelli, *The Prince*, trans. Luigi Ricci, revised E.R.P. Vincent (New York: Random House, Inc., 1950), p.21.

we perform as individuals will determine how we perform as a nation." [5]

How we perform as concerned citizens does affect the nation. If we allow corruption to go unchallenged, we have only ourselves to blame. If we abuse our leadership authority, we will pay the consequences. Likewise, if we ignore the leadership potential that sits right in front of us, we neglect the opportunity to make a difference.

Don't Miss Your Opportunity

You can help to reshape the world with your leadership contribution. It starts with a transformational process—a process of empowerment involving three main tenets:

1. Becoming a top-ranking leader is a process based on succeeding in smaller leadership roles.

Maybe you don't think you have what it takes to be a leader. Maybe you're not involved in any organizations, and all you do is play the role of parent or employee. Believe me, those roles are probably the hardest and most important leadership roles that exist. They're the roles extraordinary leadership is built upon.

Besides, some of the people who made the greatest impact in our nation began their leadership careers in small, unimpressive roles at local levels.

2. "One person can matter . . . a citizen can matter in this country." [6]

In America, potential leaders have many opportunities to practice and learn leadership—in schools, sports, local politics and volunteer and civic organizations. You have the opportunity to leave a legacy of change. But the choice to make that

---

[5] Quoted from Sheila Murray Bethel, *Making a Difference: Twelve Qualities That Make You a Leader* (New York: G.P. Putnam's Sons, 1990), p. 32.

[6] Norman Lear, as quoted by Warren Bennis, *On Becoming A Leader* (New York: Addison-Wesley Publishing Company, Inc., 1989), p. 25.

contribution is yours, and yours alone. Let me give you a few examples of people who thought they weren't doing anything spectacular.

Norman Lear, a well-known producer, screenwriter and director, learned at a young age—from his grandfather—that one person can make a difference. When Lear was about nine years old he noticed his grandfather liked to write letters. He was so fascinated with this unusual pastime that his grandfather began reading all his letters to him. Lear was amazed to realize that his grandfather was writing to the President. He would send notes of encouragement, concern and even disagreement. But what amazed Lear even more was that the President wrote back to his grandfather. [7]

Another person who made a difference was a young mother named Candy Lightner. After a drunk driver caused her daughter's needless death, Candy turned her anger into action. She wanted to do something to prevent similar tragedies, and to do that she and four other friends started MADD—Mothers Against Drunk Driving. Through her dedication to giving positive meaning to her daughter's death, MADD now has 360 chapters in 47 states and four countries. A National Commission Against Drunk Driving was launched because of Lightner's efforts, and more than 400 new laws were passed. One person *can* make a difference. [8]

In Cleveland, Ohio the school dropout rate was 49%, and Alfred Tutela, the school superintendent, wanted to do something about it. He believed education was the only way for young people to succeed in the world, and his vision was for them to realize just how valuable an

[7] Bennis, *On Becoming A Leader,* p. 35.
[8] Adapted from Sheila Murray Bethel, *Making A Difference,* (New York: G.P. Putnam's Sons, 1990), p. 14-15.

asset education was. So he instituted a plan for rewarding students for their grades.

Students in grades seven through twelve received $40 for every A, $20 for every B and $10 for every C. Each child's money was deposited into an account in his or her name and held until graduation. After graduation they could take up to eight years to use the money for either college or job training. With incentive like that a seventh grader who made straight A's through school could earn more than $1,000.

The students liked the idea so much Tutela took the plan to a group of influential community leaders, who then raised $5 million to fund the program. Now, other cities in the United States are contacting Tutela for more information about his plan.[9] An ordinary educator helped make some extraordinary changes that would affect generations to come. Who says one person can't make a difference?

3. We can safeguard ourselves from the leadership vacuum by becoming transformed and by assuring that the empowerment principles of leadership are evident in our lives.

It's time we discovered the power of the average person. You and I are the leaders who will reclaim America as a great nation. To prepare ourselves for that job, we must be sure our lives reflect the 10 principles of great leadership: inspired vision, commitment, education, organization, decisiveness, ethics, personal power, good communication, innovation and perseverance and tenacity. When we become examples that people will *want* to follow, we'll begin to make lasting impacts on the world around us.

I'm convinced that together we can make beautiful music and take hold of the vision for extraordinary leadership. This book can be the way to do just that. I've dedicated a chapter to each one

---

[9] Ibid, p. 25-26.

of the principles, explaining the reasons behind them and providing helpful strategies for making them realities in your life. I firmly believe self-empowerment is the crucial first step to great leadership. So if you will turn with me to the next chapter, we will begin by taking that step.

2

EMPOWERMENT PRINCIPLE #1
Leaders Pursue an Inspired Vision

"O World, thou choosest not the better part!
It is not wisdom only to be wise,
And on the inward vision close the eyes,
But it is wisdom to believe the heart.
Columbus found a world, and had no chart,
Save one that faith deciphered in the skies;
To trust the soul's invincible surmise
Was all his science and his only art."

—*George Santayana* [10]

"Where there is no vision, the people perish."

—*Proverbs 29:18, Authorized Version.*

---

[10] George Santayana, *The Works of George Santayana* (Triton Edition; New York: Charles Scribner's Sons, 1936), I, p. 216.

The Power Behind a Vision

Henry Ford had a mission that was as important to him as life itself. It was what he thrived on. He didn't care who laughed at him, how many times he failed or what risks were involved. Ford believed the automobile would make a greater impact on the world than any other invention because it would be the transportation method of the future.

When Ford focused on his vision, he didn't just imagine building *a* car, or *x* number of cars. He envisioned producing an automobile the average person could afford. Once he accomplished that he believed he could facilitate a transportation explosion.

Henry Ford wanted a long-lasting result that made a difference in the world. He had inspired vision.

Lessons from Ford

Long ago, organizations and businesses discovered from Ford's example that before they would see results, they had to have clear perceptions of what they wanted to accomplish. That didn't mean just projecting goals and objectives. It meant establishing common, strategic visions worth pursuing.

In other words, leaders and followers had to strive with as much fervor as Ford to accomplish their missions. It's time all of us learned some lessons from Ford and realized we, too, must have such visions.

If you are going to take on a leadership position in your work place or you decide you want to pursue some other leadership role in your community, you must have vision. Even if you believe the *only* leadership role you will hold in your life is as a parent, you still need to have an inspired vision. I believe a person's or organization's success depends on ordinary people learning the importance of and mastering the steps for creating visions. That's why establishing visions is foremost in my principles for leadership empowerment.

Empowerment Principle #1:
A person's primary act of leadership is creating and pursuing a vision significant not only to him or her, but also to the whole organization.

Creating Visions That Matter

Author and organizational consultant Peter Block says, "The inmates actually run the prison."[11] He's right. Even though security guards and wardens have "control" over inmates, the prisoners usually outnumber the authorities. That mathematical difference can mean a great deal of difference in the balance of power. The prisoners essentially have a choice whether or not to follow the rules. A little combined effort on their part can bring about changes in the prison system. And, in many instances, revolting inmates have proven the irony in prison control. For example, the correction officials can institute rehabilitative work programs all they want, but if the prisoners refuse to take part in them, rehabilitation is hopeless.

What does this have to do with leadership? If the vision matters only to the leaders, then they have limited power. The "little people" are the source of the rest of that power. They will put forth their best effort only if they are pursuing something that matters to them.

Consider a neighborhood watch program, for example. One or two people may have the inspiration to start such a program, but without the support and commitment of several more

---

[11] Peter Block, *The Empowered Manager* (San Francisco: Jossey-Bass Publishers, 1987), p. 48.

neighbors the program won't work. Everyone in the community has to buy into the vision for a safer environment; otherwise, they're not going to participate. The same is true for nearly every other leadership situation.

Sure, it's possible for leaders to filter out those people who won't do the work. But the problem will continue to arise if leaders don't create visions that are important to the entire organization. The key is: Extraordinary leadership requires people to create and avidly pursue visions of significance.

Why Such Concern About Visions?

People with vision have much more credibility than those without it. An inspired vision is a person's most profound expression of identity and desire. When leaders reveal their visions, they reveal themselves. How? They transmit their personal values. In other words, visions allow people to glimpse how leaders feel about their work, community and world. Visions define their desires and dreams. This is important because followers need to know what type of person they're depending on and looking up to.

Assume for a moment you're the leader of an environmental protection group in your city. You're concerned about the affects on the environment of non-biodegradable products, especially disposable diapers because they take up to 500 years to decompose. You begin advocating that they should be banned.

What is your vision? Is it just to ban disposable diapers? No, that's merely a goal, and as you will read later, goals and visions are two different things. Your inspired vision should express your strong values concerning environmental conservation. A more focused vision then would read: Saving and improving the environment should take precedence over convenience.

Since that vision clearly establishes where you stand as an individual, it will be much easier for you to become personally associated with the mission of the environmental group.

In this way, inspired visions work as transmitters of our values. However, they also transmit our desires for a particular future. Leaders have a unique opportunity to help create the future. For example, an environmental group leader can facilitate major changes aimed at prolonging the existence of a healthy earth. A Boy Scout leader can inspire members of his troop to become the great leaders of our country. If you desire a particular future, you can make it become reality. Determine what kind of results you want, and establish a clear vision.

Having a clear vision means you will refuse to let circumstances dictate your history. Instead, you will personally contribute to directing your part of the world. As a result, in some small way, you will also direct the rest of the world.

What Happens When There Is No Vision?

I've discovered through my experience the absence of vision results in three leadership problems.

1. Dependency

The most crippling of all leadership sicknesses is dependency. People without clear visions lose their freedom to act as self-governing individuals. Instead, they forfeit their own desires and rely on other people to guide them into the future. They allow others to set their goals and make their decisions.

2. Fear

Leaders who refuse to create visions often fear failure. They don't want to risk embarking on missions that might not succeed, and they don't want to risk the consequences of being wrong. To avoid this they either "steer a new course with each shift in the wind" or let someone else create the direction.

3. Lost Accountability

Leaders without visions also force accountability upon others because they lack the courage to accept responsibility for their or their organization's actions. When leaders give up accountability, they give up control. Once control is gone it's difficult to focus an organization on a common mission and manage its destiny.

I want to help you avoid becoming entrapped by any of these problems. To do that I want to first encourage you to seek yourself—know exactly what it is you thrive on. Throughout this book I've included personal workshops relating to the principles I believe are most important for leaders of the future. If you're serious about making a difference in your community and your life, these self-exploration workshops can help you hone your skills.

I've stressed how creating an inspired vision is crucial to the leadership role. The only way to establish an effective vision is to determine where you stand. What is important to you personally? Take a moment to participate in the following empowerment workshop.

EMPOWERMENT WORKSHOP

Define the future you want for yourself, your workplace or any other areas of your life. By writing down your dreams, you will force yourself to focus more clearly on what's important to you.

What Creating Visions Can Do for You As a Leader

We've touched on what can happen if leaders have no vision, now let's focus on the *benefits* of creating one. Vision-making provides leaders a sense of freedom. But what kind of freedom are we talking about? It's more than the liberty to pursue what you consider worthwhile. It's having the opportunity to reach for the "unreachable." Below, I've listed the three main areas in which having clear, inspired visions help leaders experience a deep sense of independence.

35

1. *Visions permit us to explore unknown frontiers and take risks.*

Have you ever dreamed of doing something that seemed totally unrealistic? Most likely you have. Did you go beyond that dreaming stage and create a vision to make it reality? If you haven't, you've squelched some of your freedom.

Establishing visions for dreams allows leaders to gain the confidence they need to explore the unknown. President Kennedy dreamed of sending a man to the moon. Had he not established a clear vision of that mission, our space program might never have become what it is today. By establishing a vision, Kennedy had the freedom and the opportunity to explore an unknown frontier.

Your vision may not be as grand as Kennedy's, but that's all right. If it's worthwhile to you personally, it's worth pursuing. Maybe you've dreamed of establishing a community center for the homeless. Yet you've never done any work with the homeless. Don't let that stop you. That's what visions are for—to help you break into those kinds of new frontiers.

Visions encourage people to become entrepreneurial or enterprising. They give leaders tangible missions to strive for. They give them reasons to take risks. After all, if you truly believe in your vision, you will be willing to do whatever it takes to achieve it.

An 11-year-old East St. Louis boy named Melvin Trent used his vision to break into a "new frontier." One night as he was watching television, he saw an appeal from an inner-city mission. Donations and volunteers were being solicited to help provide special holiday meals for the homeless. He thought for a long time about what he could do. After consulting with his family, he decided to ask the director of the mission how he might volunteer to help.

After school the next day, his mother drove him to the mission. The director was impressed with Melvin's

36

enthusiasm and suggested he might organize a group of his school friends to solicit specific items of food that might be used for the Thanksgiving and Christmas dinners. In the meeting it was decided that canned cranberries, green beans and sweet potatoes were the items most appropriate for these special meals.

With the approval of his teacher, Melvin got students in his class excited about helping. Publicity for the project was developed by the class and published in a weekly school information bulletin sent home to parents. The director of the mission supplied the students with badges to identify them as volunteers. Each child canvassed their neighborhoods on a designated Saturday and collected canned goods.

The following week, with the help of parents, the class delivered 15 boxes of food to the mission. Melvin had taken a risk—believing even a young boy could make a difference—he broke into a new frontier. He was willing to do what was necessary to achieve his vision. A vision, great or small, can make an incredible difference.

2. *Visions create hope.*

Most of us have a sense of hope deep within us. We hope to get married, have a family, get a raise or see world peace. I believe visions are the only way we can capture that spirit of anticipation. Visions arouse our expectations of success.

When we fail to conceptualize our visions we allow despair to override our hopes. And a leader without hope is a leader without vision.

In an era when economic uncertainty is a real concern, it's often hard for some to have visions of hope. A young woman from a poor family, Valerie Glass, refused to let despair override her life.

She had a vision of getting an education and working in an advertising firm. She paid her way through college by working in fast food restaurants.

37

After six years of struggling, she earned a degree in marketing.

Because of a downturn in the economy, upon graduation she received few interviews and no job offers. Valerie continued to support herself by working as a waitress, but she was determined to obtain a job in her field of study.

Answering want ads and sending out unsolicited resumes achieved few results. She joined a local professional communications organization and learned that several experienced professionals at each meeting were also looking for work.

After eight months and no job prospects, Valerie would not allow her discouragement to turn into despair. On the advice of a former professor, she enrolled in a part-time, unpaid internship with a small advertising firm. She did well working with an experienced account executive.

On Monday of the fourth week of her internship, the president of the firm asked to see her. He explained that her supervisor was leaving at the end of the week and offered her a full-time position—taking over her supervisor's accounts. She accepted the challenge and soon proved her competence.

One young woman created a vision. Although discouraged at times, she never gave up hope. She pursued her vision until it became a reality.

3. Visions function as accountability factors.

I've already mentioned how neglecting to create visions allows leaders to cast off responsibility, but let's look at it from a personal perspective. Visions are reflections of our values. They force us to hold ourselves accountable for maintaining the values we profess. In other words, visions work as the gauges other people use to evaluate leaders' actions and check whether those actions mirror the leaders' values.

38

Visions force leaders to be personally accountable, but they also keep them from hiding under a pile of insulation. We all have a tendency to insulate ourselves from disappointment and failure. Effective leaders have an entrepreneurial spirit and risk disappointment for the sake of their visions.

Kevin Costner, star of the film *Field of Dreams*, described dreams the way I think people should view their visions: "I think one of the first things to go as people's lives start to go down is their dreams. Dreams should be the last thing to go—dreams are the things you go down *with*."[12] Visions are what leaders should "go down with," and effective leaders don't insulate themselves from that fall.

Goals and Objectives Versus Visions

Goals, objectives and visions are *not* synonymous. A goal is the end toward which an effort is directed.[13] That end is usually a tangible, achievable result. For example, wanting to see that a law is passed to ban disposable diapers is a goal. The new law would be the tangible result.

An objective is something toward which an effort is directed.[14] Objectives are much like the stepping stones required to reach particular goals. For instance, your environmental group may have objectives of sending petitions to all members of Congress or obtaining commitments from consumers to boycott disposable diapers.

Unlike visions, both goals and objectives are *limited* projections of what's to come. They either predict the plans for the future or extend the plans of the past. Visions, on the other hand, are indications of what we *prefer* the future to be like. They are ideals we feel are personally worth pursuing, not necessarily concrete outcomes.

---

[12] Reprinted with permission from the *Chicago Sun-Times*, © 1992.
[13] *Webster's Ninth New Collegiate Dictionary*, p. 524.
[14] Ibid, p. 814.

That sounds like visions aren't very realistic. Not true; visions are *strategic*. They are missions of importance resulting in a desired outcome. But it's important to understand, visions arc not *strategies*. Strategies are methodical plans for achieving something, and that's not what creating visions is all about.

One of the best ways I've found for distinguishing among these terms is to consider them this way. *Objectives and goals are purpose-oriented; visions are values-oriented.* Goals and objectives are much like self-imposed schedules. They're absolutely crucial to achieving results, and in Chapter 5 we will take a look at the significance of goal setting. Visions are values-oriented because they revolve around what you, the leader, see as the most critical achievement in your life or organization.

The Art of Creating a Vision

Although you may understand *why* creating and pursuing an inspired vision is crucial to your leadership effectiveness, you may not know *how* to go about doing it. In this section I'd like to focus on just that. Earlier, in the empowerment workshop, I asked you to write down your visions for the future. If you haven't already done that, it's important for you to do so. After we've gone over the criteria for creating effective visions, it may benefit you to go back and review how accurate your first attempt was.

Creating visions means knowing how to conceptualize ideas and how to predict their future affects on your leadership role. People who wish to break out of the ordinary must be able to summarize their visions in one statement and know what belongs in a vision and what does not.

Leadership consultants Warren Bennis and Burt Nanus say, "A vision is a target that beckons."[15] Knowing how to create that vision and to compel others to follow is one of the most

---

[15] Warren Bennis and Burt Nanus, *Leaders: The Strategies for Taking Charge* (New York: Harper & Row, Publishers, 1985) p. 89.

important leadership qualities. To help you develop an inspired vision, I've listed six tips below:

1. Visions must be pursued for their own sake, not for the rewards they may bring.

Leaders who pursue visions for fame, fortune or recognition are self-absorbed and greedy. Visions should reflect the contributions leaders want to make, not what they want to receive.

When Susan B. Anthony set out to emancipate women, she didn't go after the vision for personal gain. She wanted *all* women to have the right to be heard. She wanted to bring about change to better the nation, not achieve fame for herself.

Similarly, when Melvin Trent volunteered to help the inner-city mission, he wasn't seeking self-recognition. He had a vision to help brighten the holidays for people less fortunate than himself.

2. Visions should be idealistic.

Visions aren't necessarily practical. If Melvin Trent had thought about being practical, he might never have volunteered to help the mission. There are a lot of benefits to breaking away from conservatism when you're creating a vision. Working only within what is practical stifles leaders. They need to have a sense of idealism.

Idealism is one of the qualities of youth. Melvin believed he could make a difference, and he did. He didn't worry about how he was going to achieve results. He just *knew* he would—somehow, someway. If adults had as much faith as children do, we wouldn't view so many tasks as "impossible," and we'd have a lot more people making bold visions to change the world.

Visions are idealistic; they come from the heart, not the mind. Although visions may not provide us exact destinations, they will give us courses to take.

41

3. Visions should be made with long-range perspective and should serve organizations both internally and externally.

Inspired visions are created for long-term results. They serve as expectations for future success and fulfillment. In order for this to occur, visions have to meet an organization's internal needs. That is, they must provide direction and encouragement to those people working toward the mission.

But it's equally important that visions serve the organization externally. In other words, they must contribute to the overall growth and success of the unit. Otherwise, people fail to see the benefits in striving for the vision.

4. Visions must have depth.

Superficial visions never get leaders anywhere. Visions that compel others, on the other hand, have substance and intensity and bring about extraordinary results.

Visions with depth originate from the leader's heart and are thought-provoking. Remember, if a vision isn't worth pursuing, the leader will have difficulty keeping others focused on it.

Before people can effectively encourage others to follow them, they *must* have visions with personal meaning. Leon Peters, for example, was a man who had deep, personal visions that inspired others. [16]

Peters was an Armenian who lived in Fresno, California. However, when he began working half a century ago, Armenians were discriminated against in Fresno and many other American cities.

He didn't let that get in his way. He was proud of America, and he had a strong commitment to his adopted country.

Making up for his lack of a college education, Peters worked twice as hard to succeed. He believed

---

[16] Adapted from Sheila Murray Bethel, *Making a Difference: Twelve Qualities That Make You a Leader* (New York: G.P. Putnam's Sons, 1990), p. 50-51.

people should look beyond the ordinary to see how much bigger and better things actually were. He knew America was where his dreams could come true, and he had a vision of depth that allowed him to see opportunities where no one else saw them.

Peters' vision was that it was of utmost importance to be able to do something for the community and for future generations. To assure that vision became reality, he worked with the Boy Scouts of America for 50 years, strived to protect the national parks and forests of the Sierra Nevada, and established the Fresno Community Hospital.

Now people look to his example and strive to achieve the Leon S. Peters Award for outstanding community leadership, which the Fresno Chamber of Commerce awards annually.

5. *Visions must have definition.*

Have you ever gotten involved with a group that didn't have a strong vision? It can be frustrating. The group doesn't know what its true focus is and, therefore, no one knows what they stand for.

Visions with definition have meaning not just to the leaders, but to all others involved. They have clarity and specificity.

Visions of definition are free of ambiguity. People should be able to determine without doubt what they're striving to accomplish. If a vision is vague, it reflects the leader's inability to make a commitment and leaves group members confused.

I once knew a pastor of a small church in Pittsburgh, Pennsylvania, who wanted to start a street ministry. But he didn't know exactly what he wanted to provide. He couldn't decide which group of people to target, what services he wanted to focus on or how he would go about instituting it.

His inability to focus his vision left his congregation confused and disillusioned. They didn't know whether to support

43

the pastor or not, and they certainly didn't want to commit to something they were not sure of.

Visions must be definitive. That doesn't mean you have to have all the details worked out from the beginning. But it does mean the vision must be strategic, well thought-out and concrete enough for others to grasp.

6. *Visions must reflect our commitment.*

Visions reveal our commitment to the organization and to its purpose. They act as reflections of the level of responsibility we're willing to accept. That willingness to take a stand for a particular vision reinforces the leader's dedication to the organization.

Our visions are statements of our interest in the people, work and world around us. When those visions reflect our commitment, they generate long-term focus. A person who's truly committed to a project is usually in it for the long haul. A vision reflecting commitment allows us to see beyond the immediate needs of the organization. We can foresee the ideal of what we want the organization to look like in three years or even ten years.

EMPOWERMENT WORKSHOP

Review your vision statements from the earlier empowerment workshop, and ask yourself the following questions:

■ Are they being pursued for their own sake?
■ Are they idealistic?
■ Do they have long-range perspective?
■ Do they have depth?
■ Do they have definition and specificity?
■ Are they a reflection of my commitment?

If they don't meet this criteria, rewrite them. It's crucial for effective leaders to have compelling visions. Remember to follow a child's example. Be idealistic and envision something you believe is worth pursuing.

The last tip I shared with you about inspired visions concerned commitment, which I believe is the next vital empowerment principle. Commitment or lack of it has a way of weaving itself into all other aspects of leadership. In the next chapter, we will look at just how important commitment is and take some time to determine where leaders most often fall short.

3

EMPOWERMENT PRINCIPLE #2
Leaders Are Firmly Committed

"Intensity coupled with commitment is magnetic. And these intense personalities [of leaders] do not have to coerce people to pay attention; they are so intent on what they are doing that, like a child completely absorbed with creating a sand castle in a sandbox, they draw others in." [17]

[17] Warren Bennis and Burt Nanus, *Leaders: The Strategies For Taking Charge* (New York: Harper & Row, Publishers, 1985), p. 28.

True Commitment:
The Act of the Will

In June 1953, I committed an act of will. I married Dorothy
Carmichael. I knew as I repeated my vows to her I wasn't
always going to feel the way I did at that moment. For our
marriage to last a lifetime, I knew we couldn't depend on our
feelings. We had to depend on something stronger than that.

Our minds, not our hearts, had to decide that no matter what
we faced in the future, we intended to stay together. Feelings are
erratic. They can fade or disappear over time, but the human will
has much more stamina and balance. That's what a commitment
to marriage is all about. People who wish to become extraordinary leaders must realize that same kind of steadfast commitment
is a vital quality of leadership.

True commitment is more than just verbal compliance with
an inspired vision. It's more than saying "I do" and hoping to
live happily ever after. For leaders, it's more than merely
consenting to follow visions to which they are not really
dedicated. Some people believe others don't notice whether
leaders are truly committed to their roles or to the visions
they're pursuing.

A leader's actions are clear indicators of where his or her
heart is. Insincerity in leadership will reveal itself at one point
or another. You and I both know that most people won't follow
leaders who don't walk their talk. That's hypocrisy, and a lack
of commitment is one of the surest indicators of a hypocritical
leader.

Empowerment Principle #2:
Leaders who are genuinely and firmly committed in what they and the organization are doing display the difference between poor and effective leadership.

What Is Genuine Commitment?

The word genuine implies that something or someone is authentic. With leaders, it means they're free from hypocrisy or pretense. In other words, no disguises, internal or external, hinder the leader's capabilities. Ordinary people who wish to become extraordinary leaders know the importance of having a firm, genuine commitment, and realize they must live by two major tenets:

1. Committed leaders resist the attitude that fosters a lack of commitment.

Even though we're experiencing a great surge toward the new ethic, in which workers are demanding more than just fair pay for a day's work, we still have a serious problem with the general work attitude. A 1983 Public Agenda Forum [18] revealed that many people have a tendency to withhold effort from their jobs. Apparently there's a disturbing difference between the number of hours people work and the amount of quality work produced. For example, half of all workers surveyed revealed they don't put any more effort into their jobs than what is *minimally* required. And according to the U.S. government, in 1989 our nation had the smallest gain in worker productivity since 1982. [19]

What's behind this kind of attitude? Many people don't practice good time management habits. Many don't have

---

[18] Daniel Yankelovich & Associates, *Work and Human Values* (New York: Public Agenda Foundation 1983), pp. 6-7 as reported by Bennis and Nanus, *Leaders*, p. 7.

[19] "Workers' Productivity Sees Slight Increase," *High Point Enterprise*, February 2, 1990.

anything at their jobs they feel is worthy of commitment. But I believe the main reason for this attitude is "mirroring." People are reflecting what they see in their leaders. They're simply modeling poor examples. If a leader has an indolent attitude, you can bet the followers do.

Extraordinary leaders refuse to allow themselves to fall into the trap of complacency, which fosters such an attitude among others. Complacent leaders are leaders who give in to smugness and mediocrity. Once they get to that point, they become indifferent, halfhearted and willing to settle for second best.

If you're serious about becoming a leader who makes a difference, you have to avoid becoming a victim of attitude. One of the best ways to do this is to steer clear of those who have attitude problems. Actor Henry Fonda once said a thoroughbred horse never looks at the other racehorses. It just concentrates on running the fastest race it can. [20]

Leaders need to follow similar advice. Be aware of watching and socializing with people who have poor attitudes. Complacency is contagious; it's easy to get wrapped up in another person's complaints. But if you forget about looking at the other "horses" around you, you will be able to keep up your race.

2. Committed leaders don't just talk about doing something, they do it.

Have you ever been around people who talked about all kinds of great ideas but never followed through? Leaders who lack self-confidence or clear vision are most often the victims of this syndrome. They can't seem to get their minds out of the thinking mode and into the action mode.

I once knew a college student who was like this. He always had innovative ideas for improving programs on campus, and his career goals were challenging and

---

[20] As quoted by Denis Waitley and Reni L. Witt, *Soundings* . . . , Volume D, Number 2.

exciting. The only problem was his ideas kept changing. He would continually shift his focus from one idea to another from month to month.

Since he was still in college, I gave him the benefit of the doubt, assuming he was going through some discovery processes and needed to explore several different options.

However, I happened to see this young man a few years after his graduation. Unfortunately he hadn't changed. He still couldn't make up his mind about anything, and he hadn't followed through on any of his ideas. He rattled off several more ideas to me. Again I felt most of them had great potential. But I knew if he didn't do something about the way he was handling his life, he would never actually accomplish any of the things he felt were worthwhile.

Most people who fall into this trap do so out of fear. They fear making wrong decisions, taking risks, failing and even having silly ideas. Once they become paralyzed by such fears, they never get beyond the idea-making stage.

As a musician, I've heard many other musicians expound on how well they could perform. My experience has proven to me that outstanding musicians don't need to tell you how good they are. They just pick up their instruments and play, demonstrating their commitment to their art.

Like good musicians, extraordinary leaders know the value in following through on their ideas. They understand how their own commitment fosters increased commitment from their followers, provides a security base for others and helps improve their credibility.

Leaders who intend to make a difference confront fear head on. They don't allow themselves to speak shallow, empty words about supposed commitment nor do they allow their ideas to become passing thoughts. They do everything possible to assure their lives reflect their level of commitment and to see their ideas become reality.

52

An ordinary Canadian fireman proved his commitment by putting his ideas to the test and making sure that action resulted from his efforts. He became an extraordinary leader in fire safety education.

David Guilbault was an inspector at Ottawa Fire Prevention Bureau when he pulled a lifeless 18-month-old girl from her crib during a fire. The experience agonized him, yet it sparked an idea to help prevent it from happening again.

He believed children were not being adequately educated about fire safety, so he wrote a play called *Get Out Alive*. His department didn't have the funds to take the play into the school systems. Guilbault didn't let his idea get tossed to the side. He took the initiative to see that this play was provided for children.

He spoke at a Kiwanis Club luncheon about his idea, and left with a $35,000 check. He went to Omni Entertainment in Toronto, shared his vision and left with Sparky, a $13,000 remote-control dog who rides a tricycle. Guilbault was thrilled with the robot because he had discovered through research that children retain 80% of what a robot says.

Along with Sparky, three other firefighters and four children from the audience, Guilbault performed the play in 125 schools across Ontario. Since then, Guilbault learned that a young boy credited the play for teaching him about fire safety. The child successfully led his two-year-old sister out of their burning house.

Now the play has been made into a video and distributed to more than 60 fire departments worldwide.[21] Because Guilbault remained committed, he became an extraordinary leader not just to his community and fire department, but to children worldwide.

---

[21] Charles Lewis, "Escaping fire: Tragedy sparked safety program," *Ottawa Citizen*, October, 11, 1989.

The Ingredients of Success

It's not a coincidence that committed leaders are the ones who succeed. After all, committed leaders are willing to do what's necessary to achieve their visions. When I think of people with true commitment, I consider people like my friend, Nido Qubein, one of the nation's leading business consultants and speakers.

> Nido came to this country when he was 18 years old—an ordinary Lebanese immigrant. He had $50 to his name, and he knew practically no English. Now that second language is the means for his livelihood and has helped him become a millionaire before age 40.

> Nido knew the main ingredient of success was an unfaltering, sacrificial commitment. He committed everything he had to becoming a successful speaker and consultant. He worked 12-14 hours a day, practiced his speaking until he was hoarse, and invested all his income in his business. He knew that rewards didn't come without sacrifices, and his vision was so strong he could easily forfeit what many of us consider comforts to fulfill it.

> What makes Nido so unique is that immediately upon reaching a goal, he sets another one. To this day, he sacrifices enormously because he's committed to obtaining his visions and being the best leader he can be.

The truth is: Ordinary people cannot hope to see themselves, their organizations or others become extraordinary if they're reluctant to make sacrifices. A full commitment is what gives a person the *right* to earn the title of leader.

Jesus Christ, who many consider the greatest leader of all time, knew what kind of obligation leaders would face when he said, "Much is required from those to whom much is given, for their responsibility is greater." [22] People who are given the job

---

[22] *The Living Bible*, Luke 12:48.

of leading others are *given* a great deal of power and responsibility, and with that comes high expectations.

No one finds much credibility in a leader who's unwilling to forfeit what's necessary to make the organization succeed or make the vision reality. A deep sense of dedication is what's vital for leaders to remain committed. I've discovered that people earn their leadership recognition through credibility by following three rules:

1. Leaders are dedicated to people.

Leaders have an obligation to guide people with enthusiasm because those people are their most important resources. If leaders are not dedicated to those under their direction, they will never know the joy of true leadership. Leadership is not about gaining position and prestige; it's about empowering other people to join you on an exciting mission.

To do that, leaders need to have a vested interest in others. An honest concern for the well-being of co-workers makes the job more meaningful. This type of dedication to followers isn't just socializing that decreases productivity like some people think. Rather it's the kind of participation that fosters even greater job satisfaction.

The way leaders act toward others is the best way to determine their level of dedication. A condescending attitude toward workers obviously doesn't reflect a high level of dedication. But an energetic, positive attitude establishes solid commitment.

2. Leaders set good examples.

As a child, did you ever have a hero? Most of us did at one time or another. Those heroes were our role models, our examples, the people we valued and respected. We remember that whenever we attempted to model after our heroes, we were trying to do the same kind of good they did.

When I was a teenager, my hero was Bob Schupp, my high school music teacher. He set out to revitalize

55

our school music program. He worked tirelessly during, before and after school hours to help us improve our musicianship and appreciation of music. He encouraged more and more students to become involved in band, choir, glee clubs and small ensembles. He took us to orchestra concerts, opera performances and music contests. He helped me to discipline myself toward excellence in saxophone performance and as an aspiring student conductor. Because of him I decided to study music in college. In my career as a music teacher, I can remember trying to be like him by giving freely of my time to help my students.

It's important to realize leaders who set good examples help bring out the best in other people. Ralph Waldo Emerson said, "What you are speaks so loudly that I cannot hear what you say." That statement couldn't be more true. Our example says much more than our words do, especially if it's bad. Leaders who fail to act as good examples remind me of a television commercial aired with the intent to fight the war against drugs.

In the commercial a father is yelling at his son while holding a bag of drug paraphernalia. He's demanding to know where his son learned to use it. The boy looks up angrily at his father and yells back, "I learned it from you!" The message of the commercial hits hard.

Apparently this father had talked to his son about not using drugs, but his example spoke louder than his words. Had the father been truly committed to keeping his son drug-free he himself would be drug-free. His talk would have been supported by his walk.

Consider what the actions of this small, bent, old woman say.

Walking the streets of a poverty-stricken city in India, this woman saw a man lying in a gutter. Nobody would go near him because he was covered with vermin and reeked from disease. But she did. She even knelt down next to him and started cleaning him. The man was so overwhelmed by her actions he asked why she was helping him. That little old woman, whom we know as Mother Teresa of Calcutta, said simply, "Because I love you."

Had she told the man as she walked by that she loved him, he wouldn't have believed her. Instead, she proved with her actions before she ever spoke the words that she truly had a genuine love for him. [23]

Mother Teresa has such a burning passion for helping the poor and destitute she has dedicated much of her life to them. Even now at 80 years old she continues to walk the streets of Calcutta ministering to people most of us would never pass within ten feet of—people festering with disease and covered with filth.

Her example has encouraged many others to dedicate their lives to serving the poor. She has also helped to establish the worldwide Sisters of Charity, which has brought increased recognition to the issue of poverty. Because of her strong commitment, Mother Teresa has truly become an extraordinary leader in the mission against poverty.

The key to setting a good example is remembering that people emulate the actions, attitudes and emotions of their leaders. You don't need to be a hero or a Mother Teresa to be an effective leader. But your example must impact others enough that they will see the value in following you.

3. Leaders accept responsibility.

Earlier I mentioned how effective leaders are willing to accept the responsibility of their positions. That means they must understand they are the ones held accountable for what

---

[23] Adapted from Sheila Murray Bethel, *Making A Difference* (New York: G.P. Putnam's Sons, 1990), pp. 268-269.

happens under their leadership. The buck has to stop some-where, and 99% of the time it stops with the leader.

Extraordinary leaders know the value of delegating authority, but they also know they're ultimately responsible for the results of that delegation. This kind of accountability should not be viewed as a burden; it's a reflection of the leader's confidence and courage. It takes great courage to accept responsibility for mistakes in judgement.

Effective leaders know when they're given leadership power, they're required to prove themselves worthy of it. Placing the blame for any problems on others is the easiest way to reveal insecurity. And leaders who want to make an impact know sacrificing the comfort of security comes with the title.

The Price of Leadership Is Sacrifice

Extraordinary leaders realize the price they pay for leadership responsibility is measured in sacrifice. People can't barter for leadership; they must earn it by sacrificing. To sacrifice means to give up one thing for the sake of something else. Effective leaders give up a great deal for the sake of their visions. I believe if you're serious about becoming a leader, you must be serious about making four crucial sacrifices:

1. Leaders sacrifice time.

Becoming a leader doesn't happen overnight. It's a develop-mental process that can take months, even years. Potential leaders must be willing to take the time to hone those skills that will make them extraordinary leaders. Often that time must be sacrificed on a daily basis.

If you are willing to make a long-term commitment to pursuing a vision, you can't be a clock-watcher. Committed leaders don't know the meaning of a 40-hour work week. They're willing to sacrifice whatever time is necessary for achieving their goals and getting the work done.

2. *Leaders sacrifice ego.*

There's no room for power-hungry, self-glorifying people in extraordinary leadership. When you commit to becoming a leader, you leave your ego at home.

Extraordinary leaders don't try to reach goals and pursue visions that coddle their pride. Instead, they gain a deep sense of satisfaction from relinquishing selfish attitudes.

True leadership is not about ego; it's about humility. It takes a great deal of humility to forsake personal glory for the success of the organization. It takes even more to hand over authority and empower others to be more successful than you.

3. *Leaders sacrifice power.*

Extraordinary leaders do not struggle to gain leadership positions just so they can control other people's lives. The kind of power leaders should strive for is not power for its own sake. Instead, it's the power that enables them to accomplish personal and organizational goals, to achieve the vision.

Positional power is the type of power that gets many leaders into trouble. This is when people take advantage of the authority and access they have. They bask in the glory of gaining supremacy.

But authority doesn't come this way. Leaders receive authority by gaining *personal* power. In Chapter 8, we'll focus specifically on what personal power is and how it benefits the extraordinary leader.

4. *Leaders sacrifice assurance.*

It's important to realize being a leader is risky business. People need to understand that leadership positions are **not** comfortable. They can't be assured of success or popularity. People only become extraordinary when they refuse to give up, regardless of the circumstances.

Aviator Charles Lindbergh was such a person. He was so committed to his vision of flying across the ocean he risked his life to achieve it. He navigated his expeditions in this country using only the terrain and waterways, and he hung onto the hope that his "washing-machine" engine would carry him over the sea. Now that's sacrificing assurance!

EMPOWERMENT WORKSHOP

What kind of specific sacrifices could you make that would increase your level of commitment?

Commitment Conquers Obstacles

Being committed to an overriding purpose enables people to overcome obstacles. A firmly dedicated person is less likely to succumb to fear, which is one of the two most crippling leadership obstacles. I've found that leaders are most afraid of these three things:

Failure

No one likes to fail, and leaders certainly don't, since they are held accountable for failure. But everyone knows success doesn't come without some failure. Charles F. Kettering said:

> *"Virtually nothing comes out right the first time.*
> *Failures, **repeated** failures, are finger posts on the*
> *road to achievement. The only time you don't fail*
> *is the last time you try something, and it works. One*
> *fails forward toward success."* [24]

Rejection

At times, rejection can seem worse than failure. Leaders often fear their ideas or decisions will be considered silly or wrong, and they will lose the support of their followers. But rejection

---

[24] Charles F. Kettering, "Points To Ponder," *Reader's Digest*, May 1989, p. 47.

builds character. And character is often the distinctive feature of extraordinary people.

People laughed at Alexander Graham Bell. They snorted when Margaret Thatcher thought she could lead England. But Bell and Thatcher each stuck to their guns. Now we wouldn't know what to do without the telephone, and England was successfully led by the first woman in Parliament for more than 11 years.

So what does this say about dealing with rejection? Remain committed. Walt Disney had a way of handling rejection that really inspired me. He would ask 10 people what they thought of one of his ideas. If they were unanimous in their rejection, he would immediately start working on it.[25] Now that's taking rejection and turning it into success.

Change

In this fast-paced world, it's no wonder leaders often fear change. One day they may feel confident in their jobs, and the next they may wonder if they're going to be replaced by a machine or eliminated altogether because of downsizing. Extraordinary leaders must be willing to risk change. They don't succumb to the fear of change; instead, they use it to their advantage. They always look at it as an opportunity for improvement.

Battling Discouragement

The second most crippling obstacle leaders face is discouragement and frustration—letting themselves wallow in self-pity. Committed leaders don't even have the word pity in their dictionaries. Most often people become discouraged and frustrated because they aren't seeing progress, or they've lost a major source of emotional or monetary support.

I knew a man who wanted to open a sandwich shop in a small town but succumbed to discouragement. He became increasingly frustrated because his local financiers

---

[25] Denis Waitley, *10 Seeds of Greatness* (Grand Rapids, Michigan: Baker Book House, 1983), p. 36.

began doubting the success of the venture. Eventually they all withdrew their support.

The man didn't bother trying to find other financiers because he'd already allowed himself to be eaten up with frustration. He believed because he had lost the emotional support of his neighbors as well as the financial support necessary to start the business there was nothing to do but give up.

Extraordinary leaders don't let frustration get the best of them. Alexander Graham Bell certainly didn't. No one other than his immediate family supported him, and it took a long time for him to see progress. But he had enough commitment and self-esteem to survive. He was so convinced his inventions would work he even dedicated a great deal of time to establishing the production of them. He refused to invent something that would sit on a shelf in a laboratory; he wanted his ideas to be *used*. Ultimately, he established Bell Laboratories to see that they were.

One of the best examples of an ordinary person who overcame discouragement and frustration to become an extraordinary leader is Wilma Monroe. Wilma was an unwed mother of two living on welfare in a public housing project in downtown Chicago. She was an eighteen-year-old high school dropout supporting her children with a minimum wage job at a fast food restaurant.

Wilma had every reason to be discouraged but she refused to let her situation get the best of her. She knew education was the only way out of her predicament so she enrolled in a night school course to help her prepare for the high school equivalency examination. She passed the exam on her first attempt. With encouragement from her work supervisor, she enrolled in the evening associate degree program in business at a nearby community college. Working a 40-hour week, taking night classes and raising two children was difficult, but having barely enough money each month to cover day care, college expenses and basic necessities added even more stress to her life. Wilma, however, was determined not to give in to discouragement.

In three-and-one-half years of working full-time and taking classes part-time, she completed her associate degree. During this period she was promoted to a supervisory position and encouraged to further her education. She enrolled in Chicago State University and set a new goal of completing a degree in accounting.

Finally, at age twenty-nine, Wilma graduated with a B.S. in accounting and took a higher paying job with an accounting firm. She believes the struggle with financial hardship and balancing work and family obligations to get an education was well worth the sacrifice. Although she no longer lives in the same neighborhood, she returns regularly to speak to students about the importance of staying in school and getting an education. She has become an excellent role model for these youngsters.

What makes Wilma an extraordinary leader is commitment. She had a vision of educating herself. Once she put that vision into action she was on her way to success. She didn't have to become a famous financial expert. She was just an ordinary unwed, welfare mother who took the initiative and brought about extraordinary results in her life and in the lives of many young people in an impoverished neighborhood.

I believe extraordinary leaders are people like Wilma who start out as ordinary people struggling to make a difference in their lives and in the world. Commitment is clearly a critical factor in leadership. David Guilbault was committed to seeing his life-saving play in the school systems. Charles Lindbergh was committed to flying across the ocean.

And Wilma Monroe was 100% committed to getting an education, which moves me into the next empowerment principle necessary for leaders. In the next chapter you will discover how education is vital to strengthening leaders for the long haul.

4

EMPOWERMENT PRINCIPLE #3
Leaders Promote Education

"The great aim of education is not knowledge but action."

—Herbert Spencer [26]

"What you learn with just the mind is quickly forgotten; what you learn when you are also emotionally involved remains imprinted in the nervous system; and the first task of education is involvement, not mere learning."

—Sydney Harris [27]

---

[26] Reprinted from Lloyd Cory, *Quotable Quotes* (Wheaton, IL: Victor Books, 1985), p. 112.
[27] Ibid, p. 112.

Making a Difference Through Education

A vast difference exists between the processes of training and educating. Unfortunately, few people seem to know it. For you, the distinction can mean the difference in remaining an ordinary person and becoming an extraordinary leader.

Every year people who can't write their names, balance their checkbooks or read the backs of cereal boxes graduate from high schools and colleges. Did you know that 61% of American adults can't locate Massachusetts on a map? That United States' schools graduate 700,000 students yearly who can't read at fourth-grade level? [28]

The truth is: As a nation we don't approach education the way we should. Instead of concentrating on what's vital for knowledge, which is *a broad range of understanding,* we're inundated with a litany of facts.

This problem is not just affecting our children, it's affecting you and me. That's why I believe it's especially crucial for leaders to understand education as an empowerment principle. To become an extraordinary leader, you need to approach education as a personal mission of self-improvement.

---

[28] Anita Manning, "Are we a nation of nitwits?" *USA Today,* February 13, 1989, pp. 1D-2D.

Empowerment Principle #3:
Extraordinary leaders promote education because it facilitates the personal change necessary for leadership improvement.

Let's take a moment to look at the words training and educating and determine the definition of each.

According to Webster's Dictionary, *training* is: the process of forming someone or something by instructing, disciplining or drilling.

In other words, training is simply "schooling" people. It's covering certain material in a passive manner or teaching people how to do particular tasks by rote.

Educating, on the other hand, is: the process of persuading a person to feel, believe or act in a desired way.

It's a process of assuring that people are thinking and mentally recording in a way that enables them to gain a personal understanding of certain information.

Historian Henry Adams made a wise statement long ago concerning education. He said, "Nothing in education is so astonishing as the amount of ignorance it accumulates in the form of inert facts." [29]

Education is not incorporating 10 new techniques into your leadership style or memorizing strategies for solving problems. Those are merely inert facts. Instead, it's the process of prodding our minds to unfold and think about new concepts. Training can occur without too much thought, but it's impossible for education to take place without hard, concentrated, analytical thinking.

Becoming Your Own Think Tank

Critical thinking is what propels people forward into extraordinary leadership. Effective leaders are critical thinkers

---

[29] Henry Adams, *The Education of Henry Adams* as quoted by Henry Davidoff, *The Pocketbook Of Quotations* (New York: Pocket Books, 1952), p. 75.

because they realize analytical abilities are one of the greatest tools they could ever have. Instead of filling themselves with basic facts, they strive to *understand* the whys behind the facts.

When people think in a meaningful way they work to comprehend and remember what's necessary to improve their skills. To understand the value of critical thinking, let's take a look at the difference between the terms *thinking* and *critical thinking*.

The word *critical* refers to something being indispensable, crucial or necessary. Therefore, critical thinking is a process of:

1. Determining what is indispensable information.

2. Retaining what is crucial.

3. Knowing when it's necessary to use that information.

Effective leaders who think critically refuse to play the game of "knowledge trivia." In other words, they don't seek information for information's sake. They don't memorize the five foolproof steps for getting people to do more work just so they can look good.

Instead, they want "meat and potatoes" information. They want to know *why* they should do something a certain way, *what* proof there is it works that way, and *how* they should go about trying it themselves.

People rarely retain subject matter they don't think about. That means it's difficult for leaders to improve their leadership skills without continuously *acquiring* and *applying* new knowledge. Thinking is a participative exercise; it's not something people can do passively. There's an old Chinese proverb that states:

"Tell me, I forget.
Show me, I remember.
Involve me, I understand."

To me this proverb reveals the best way we can look at critical thinking. It should be based on involvement. Leaders must be absorbed in the educational process; otherwise, they will never convince themselves personal change is beneficial.

69

The Benefits of Breaking Tradition

As children, most of us were taught the traditional way. We went to class, opened our textbooks and listened to our teachers lecture on what we could have read for ourselves. The teachers told us what we needed to know, and we supposedly learned it.

What we actually did was memorize the information until the test was over. Then we probably forgot it.

As adults, we know this is an ineffective method of education. Yet we still find ourselves attending seminars and conferences trying to learn through memorization what the speakers tell us we should and should not do. A week later, most of us have forgotten what it was we were supposed to have learned.

This is one of the main reasons I'm so against rote training. I'm not advocating that training should be totally abolished because in some educational settings it's an effective and appropriate means of learning. For instance, soldiers must be trained to handle combat situations. Children must be trained to tie their shoes and write their names.

But when it comes to leadership, you cannot hope to *just* train yourself to be better. You must educate yourself—you must become a critical thinker.

Researchers estimate we remember:

10% of what we read.

20% of what we hear.

30% of what we see.

70% of what we say. [30]

90% of what we say *and* do.

What does this imply about the way we're attempting to learn? Most of us are not going to learn anything by simply reading a book about leadership or listening to a speaker. Only when we can personalize information we've read or heard and

---

[30] Robert M. Gagne, *The Conditions of Learning* (New York: Holt, Rinehart, and Winston), 1965 as quoted from Judy Self, *Plain Talk About Learning and Writing Across The Curriculum* (Virginia Department of Education, 1987), p. 13.

explain it to another person in our own words have we begun to learn.

By achieving a broad range of understanding instead of just training ourselves in certain areas, we should be able to stand back and see how we've remodeled ourselves from ordinary people into extraordinary leaders.

Why Promote Learning?

The only way to generate extraordinary results is to promote learning. By educating ourselves we learn how to comprehend information that will help us set up strong foundations for moving toward leadership success. Extraordinary leaders know how vital it is to commit their time, energy and resources to facilitating proper comprehension.

By thoroughly understanding information—making it applicable to our lives —we will begin learning. But before this type of comprehension can occur, we must process knowledge in two ways:

1. We should understand it enough to logically put it into our own words.

It's easy to restate what someone else says word-for-word. After all, it doesn't take a fifth-grader long to memorize the Gettysburg Address. That's just rote learning—repeating the lines over and over again until the child can say them without thinking. The ability to recite the Gettysburg Address, then, does nothing but prove the student can memorize.

But it's a different situation for a fifth-grader to go line-by-line through the speech and understand exactly what Lincoln was saying to the American people. When a student can tell you what Lincoln meant, he or she has *learned* an important part of history.

We don't prove any kind of great leadership ability by stating verbatim someone else's strategies. We confirm our ability to comprehend and analyze information when we can express that person's ideas in a creative, personal way and follow through on them with our actions.

71

2. We should remember it because it associates personally with our lives.

How many times have you attended a meeting and realized the only information you remembered was that which associated with your life or organization? That's not uncommon. As soon as we hear information we begin to screen it—discarding what is unnecessary or irrelevant to us, and storing what is vital.

When data relates to us personally we're much more likely to remember it. For example, if I asked you to participate in a workshop on problem-solving and I gave everyone the same sample problem to work with, two weeks later you may not remember how you solved that problem.

However, if I had you work on a problem you're currently facing in your organization, you'd probably never forget how you solved it. That problem was personal to you; therefore, the solution became etched in your memory. This proves how a significant relationship exists between how well a person learns and how much the information personally associates with his or her life.

Carrying Personal Involvement into Empowerment

The emphasis in extraordinary leadership is empowerment—the process of bringing people out of a passive mode of followership into an active mode of influence. Empowered people know how to take the initiative and tackle problems, responsibilities and other people without always holding the leaders' hands.

To empower people, leaders replace traditional, inefficient training strategies with *educating-to-learn* strategies. Educating-to-learn is a method of helping yourself and others become articulate, knowledgeable leaders through critical thinking. Below are what I believe to be the four major educating-to-learn strategies:

Writing

Most people remember those things they write down better than if they rely solely on their memories. Have you ever prepared a list of items you needed from the store then inadvertently left the list at home? Even without the list you probably didn't have much trouble remembering everything. The writing process somehow ingrains information in our minds.

In seminars, attendees are often provided workbooks to encourage them to jot down notes and record important information. This isn't accidental. Seminar speakers know writing is one of the most successful methods for concentrating and analyzing. The mind processes data so fast we often can't keep up with it. The writing process helps us focus our attention.

I know business leaders who swear by this learning strategy. For example, some lawyers write abstracts of long, detailed policies they're required to know. They want to assure they understand and will remember the information.

Writing is also an effective method of brainstorming, problem-solving and strategizing. I've discovered that people who keep some type of journal to express their ideas and struggles can more quickly solve problems, come up with innovative ideas and improve their skills.

When I write down the circumstances surrounding a problem, I can focus more clearly on the real issue and all possible options for solving it. Writing about a predicament forces me to think about it critically; it forces me to internalize the situation. Usually, if I run across a similar situation later, I'm more apt to recall how I solved it. Don't forget, we remember 90% of what we say and do, and what better way to be sure we say what we need to learn than to write it down.

Applying

Application is the process of putting information into action. It's relating that which a person has learned to his or her everyday life. For example, what have you gained by memorizing the process of changing a tire if you can't put that knowledge to use and actually replace a flat tire?

The application process is a leader's testing ground. It's the point in the learning process that determines whether you've truly grasped a concept. For example, education majors in college learn a great deal from textbooks and professors about how to teach, but they can't actually test that knowledge until they're standing in front of a class full of children.

As far as any type of leadership role is concerned, you hone your skills by applying them.

Questioning

Questioning is one of the best ways to assure you're gaining the most from the information you're learning. The Greek philosopher Socrates probed his student's minds by answering questions with questions. He wanted them to discover how to solve their own problems. It proved to be an excellent method of sharpening their analytical thinking skills.

Leaders who question the information they're given can not only determine whether it's valid and significant to them, but also where they still fall short in their knowledge. Questions indicate potential problems and flaws in a person's information processing. They determine how much of the subject matter has been understood or how it will relate to that person's life or situation. Benjamin Franklin questioned every step of his experimentation with lightning and conduction. Had he not, he might never have discovered electricity.

Framing

Framing involves visualizing programs or strategies *before* they're implemented to determine how they could affect your life.

Let's say, for instance, you've heard about a method of encouraging your salespeople to increase profits. You believe this approach could produce considerable improvements in your organization. Before you attempt to use the idea, you should frame out both the positive and negative affects of the change.

In other words, imagine how the organization would run if you implemented the idea. What kind of reaction would it bring about from your sales force? What potential problems could arise? What's different about your organization than the one from which you got the idea?

By doing this you can prevent yourself from jumping into something too soon and making mistakes in judgment. Framing allows leaders to take the whole situation into consideration before they have to say, "It's too late."

The Value of Making It Personal

Extraordinary leaders know the value of the statement: Knowledge must become personal. After all, the educating-to-learn process is a strategy of taking information and applying it individually. People cannot become better leaders if they don't embark on a continuous mission to use their education in their lives.

Philosopher Andrew Murray said, "Readiness and ability for any work is not given before the work, but only through the work." Leaders can't become better leaders until they put to action the skills they've learned.

As a young naval officer, I had the opportunity to use the small sailing boats at the base where I was stationed. However, before a person could use the boats, he or she had to qualify as a "small boat sailor." At that point in my naval career I had experience driving ships at sea, but I had never been on a boat powered by wind and sail.

I wanted to qualify to use these boats, so a friend and I enrolled in a base-sponsored sailing course. For several weeks we attended class one night a week and studied sailing terminology, "rules-of-the-road" and theory. When we took the written examination we both passed with ease.

We still had to pass a practical examination, a sailing test, yet we knew nothing about actually sailing the boat. The only way we would truly understand the principles we had studied earlier was to apply our book-knowledge. Luckily, we both passed the test on our first day sailing, but that didn't mean we were educated sailors. It took several more weeks of practice before we considered ourselves true "small boat sailors."

The point to the illustration is: we were trained in sailing, but we weren't *educated* in it until we made the information personal—until we literally got out in a boat and sailed. We could have analyzed on paper over and over how to solve potential problems sailors face on the water, but the truth is, there's no way we could determine if those solutions would work until we tried them.

Educating People in Problem-Solving

Solving problems is probably one of the single, most important responsibilities of a leader. Parents constantly try to resolve problems with their children. Business leaders deal with finances and competition. Civic leaders face apathy, lack of commitment and hundreds of other things. Problem-solving is a part of life.

But we don't have to let our problems get the best of us. We can educate ourselves to handle difficulties in the most constructive manner. Below are some tips I follow to solve problems.

1. Focus on the problem not the symptom.

We often get so wrapped up in symptoms we never really see the problem. It's common for leaders to focus on what appears to be the problem and misjudge how they should handle the situation. Ultimately they never get around to dealing with the real issue.

Let's say, for example, a person in your organization who usually has been a reliable associate, has recently become chronically late and less productive. You might think the problem is laziness. But that could just be the symptom of a greater problem.

The person could be suffering from an inordinate amount of stress due to a particular project, and his or her behavior may only be a defense mechanism. Or it's possible the person

76

is having serious problems at home which are affecting behavior on the job.

Whatever the reason, leaders are responsible for determining where the real problem lies and focusing on solving it.

2. Think problems through; don't just think about them.

No one ever gets anywhere sitting around worrying *about* their problems. It's crucial that leaders discipline themselves to strategically think through their situations and act on their decisions instead of passively pondering them. It's not uncommon for ineffective leaders to let problems requiring action lie on their desks for months because they're thinking about them.

Extraordinary leaders use their critical thinking skills. They focus on the issue at hand and come up with solutions as quickly as they can.

3. Break big problems down into bite-sized chunks and deal with them individually.

People don't like to be overwhelmed. Leaders often find themselves in predicaments because they try to deal with more than they can handle.

Extraordinary leaders are strategists. They combat their difficulties by reducing them into smaller, easier-to-handle chunks. Babies learn to walk one step at a time. Leaders need to tackle problem-solving the same way: one step at a time.

4. Act in a considered way.

Effective leaders think before they act and maintain their composure when dealing with crises. Overreacting is the biggest culprit in making problems larger and more difficult to handle than they were in the first place.

The example of how test pilots are taught to handle problems in the air is the best example I know of leaders acting in a considered way. When test pilots are faced with a problem, they force themselves to ask, "Is this thing still flying?" *before* they do anything.

When Apollo II took off, its pilots got to put this approach to the test. The launch went without a hitch, but suddenly as it rose into the air the capsule was hit by a freak lightening bolt. The pilots stared wide-eyed as every warning light on the console glowed orange and red. They had an incredible urge to immediately do something, but instead they stopped and asked themselves, "Is this thing still flying?"

It was; they were still heading for the moon, their intended destination. So they started breaking down the problem into bite-sized chunks. They handled one light at a time, and eventually the console glowed the safe green again.

Those pilots were obviously well educated, not trained, in dealing with problems. They had a plan, and they followed it through. In Chapter 5 we'll talk about the importance of just that—planning. The role of organization is a vital component to extraordinary leadership. So turn with me to discover why.

5

EMPOWERMENT PRINCIPLE #4
Leaders Know the Value of Organization

"How shall I be able to rule over others when I have not full power and command over myself?"

—*Rabelais* [31]

"Failures can be divided into those who thought and never did, and those who did and never thought."

—*W.A. Nance* [32]

---

[31] Reprinted from Lloyd Cory, *Quotable Quotes* (Wheaton, IL: Victor Books, 1985), p. 344.
[32] Ibid, p. 128.

The Ways of the Ant

The Proverb says, "Go to the ant, you sluggard; consider its ways and be wise!" [33] In other words, wise people should work diligently with a plan in an organized fashion. If you've ever watched ants for any length of time, you know they aren't lazy. They get their work done.

I believe the evidence of organization in people's lives reflects more about their character than almost any other leadership quality. Few of us like to follow people who appear harried, disorderly and inefficient. We want to look up to leaders who govern their lives with as much discipline and self-control as they use in governing their organizations.

Extraordinary leaders understand the value of the axiom:

> *"For all your days prepare,*
> *And meet them ever alike:*
> *When you are the anvil, bear—*
> *When you are the hammer, strike."*

> *—Edwin Markham* [34]

The truth is effective leaders are master organizers. They triumph over disorder and poor planning to avoid the kind of hindrances that prevent them from achieving their visions. Organization and preparedness are the keys to maintaining

---

[33] *The Bible*, New International Version, Proverbs 6:6.

[34] Edwin Markham, *Preparedness*, as quoted by Louis Filler, *The Unknown Edwin Markham: His Mystery and Its Significance* (Yellow Springs, Ohio: The Antioch Press, 1966), p. 172.

credibility, respect and success. And smart leaders depend on that.

Empowerment Principle #4:
Effective leadership is most often evidenced by organization.

Personal discipline makes a difference in the way leaders are perceived. The military, for example, has a high regard for order, and they're greatly respected for it.

If it weren't for the organization and discipline that's instilled in soldiers, many more men would have lost their lives in battles. Strategic planning and solid prioritizing are the qualities that have won wars and saved lives.

The military, however, isn't the only place where organization makes an impact. People from presidents of major corporations and heads of state to United Way chairpersons and parents can turn the ordinary into the extraordinary by taking some time to improve their self-management.

The Churchill Challenge: Mastering Prioritization

Winston Churchill was a man who knew the value of organizing his life. He knew exactly what he could get done in a day, and his schedule was almost dictatorial in assuring the proper amount of work got accomplished. How did he assure himself of that? He prioritized.

The first step to empowering yourself through organization is to practice prioritizing. Unfortunately, it's also one of the most difficult leadership tasks to master. Blaise Pascal once said, "The last thing one knows is what to put first." [35] For most of us that's true. We know we should be prioritizing in our lives, but we don't know where to begin. I've discovered it begins with strict discipline. I'm not saying your life must be regimented and you can never deviate from your schedule. That's absurd. But if you're

---

[35] Reprinted from Lloyd Cory, *Quotable Quotes* (Wheaton, IL: Word Books, 1985), p. 304.

serious about becoming an extraordinary leader, you need to have a strategy for disciplining your life.

Even though some people thought Winston Churchill had a disorderly daily schedule, he was quite rigid in his routine. [36] He worked wisely so he could accomplish the most pressing tasks at hand.

After rising each morning at 8:00 he would read for four hours to keep his mind keen and abreast of current issues. Later, he had a particular portion of the morning in which he dictated his correspondence and composed speeches.

Throughout the day, if he were not required to be in London, he had scheduled times for feeding his goldfish, painting or meeting with friends and colleagues. And at 11:00 in the evening his true working day began. He would spend six to eight hours dictating to two secretaries, working in shifts, to prepare a 40 minute speech. Finally, he would retire at 2:00 or 3:00 A.M.

It's crucial for a leader to set an example by focusing his or her priorities. It's a proven fact that inappropriate or poorly established personal and professional priorities steer more people into trouble than any other aspect of leadership.

Consider the predicament in which President Richard Nixon placed himself. His involvement in the burglary of the Watergate Hotel revealed where his priorities lay.

He valued personal power and political advantage over his opponents more than providing a leadership example and following the laws of the nation he led. Those misplaced priorities were the cause of his downfall.

You may think your priorities aren't even remotely similar to Nixon's, so you have nothing to worry about. But poor prioritizing can affect a person in other ways that are just as serious.

I once knew a man named John who also stood out as a prime example of a person without priorities. John had

---

[36] William Manchester, "The Lion Caged," *American Heritage*, (XXXVIII Feb./Mar. 1987), p. 65-68.

considerable experience as an officer in a large organization. His superiors assumed, because of his level of expertise and the fact he was responsible for accomplishing tasks according to the priorities set by his current manager, he had mastered priority-setting in his own life. He had not, but he covered it up well.

When he was recognized for his outstanding leadership ability, John was promoted to a high level line position where he was responsible for a large, rather complex unit in the organization. But John was out of his element.

As a staff officer he was accustomed to supporting tasks directed and prioritized by his superiors. Suddenly, *he* was required to prioritize and provide direction for his unit. He didn't know the first thing about prioritizing and time management. As a result, he failed to assign tasks with any distinction. He simply gave everything "top priority" and placed unnecessary burdens on his subordinates.

Because none of his employees knew the relative importance of any assignment, the critical, often less attractive tasks were frequently neglected in favor of the more appealing, less important ones. Eventually, John's unit had the lowest productivity in the organization, and he lost his job.

Discovering Relative Importance

John's problem was he didn't know how to determine the relative importance of any task. And the key to properly aligning priorities is knowing how to judge what is and isn't important. But before leaders can prioritize tasks in an organization, they need to prioritize their lives.

Your personal life will carry over into your leadership role. So you need to establish your life priorities.

1. Determine your life motivation.

What one thing makes you want to continue living? What things in life motivate you to achieve your visions and goals?

2. Determine your life purpose.

What do you believe you're on this earth to do? What role will your life play in the world during the course of your lifetime? What purposes must your life fulfill?

3. Determine your personal values.

What things do you believe are important and must be a part of your life? What makes your life personally fulfilling?

If you try to prioritize your life without including all three of these areas, you will notice imbalance at some point. In Chapter 1, we talked about how a leader's vision is a reflection of his or her personal values. The same is true for priorities. When it comes to priorities, it's impossible for leaders to know what they want out of life if they don't know what's personally fulfilling to them.

```
┌─────────────────────────────────────┐
│                                      │
│       EMPOWERMENT WORKSHOP           │
│                                      │
└─────────────────────────────────────┘
```

In 25 words or less write down what you consider to be the single most important motivating factor in your life.

Then list in order of importance the 10 things in your life you consider most essential for self-fulfillment.

Are these 10 elements prioritized and congruent with your motivating factor? If not, how can you achieve that?

Peak Performance Takes Discipline

If you're serious about leadership, you have to be serious about prioritizing, and this takes enormous discipline. Ernest Newman once talked about the lives of great composers and what he said revealed the role discipline plays in their lives.

> *"The great composer does not set to work because he is inspired, but becomes inspired because he is working. Beethoven, Wagner, Bach and Mozart settled down day after day to the job in hand with as much regularity as an accountant settles down each day to his figures. They didn't waste time waiting for an inspiration."* [37]

Had these composers not been disciplined enough to sit down *regularly* to compose, they could have waited a long time for the inspiration to write. But these men had their priorities straight. They were dedicated to meeting their most important priority—composing a piece of music.

Leaders who have a sense of discipline in their lives and control their time, operate at peak performance. They're the ones who see consistent results from their efforts.

What Happens When Priorities Aren't Present?

To understand the impact of this principle more fully, let's take a look at what happens if priorities aren't present in your life. If you're like me you've given in at times—you've compromised your priorities.

Maybe you decided work was more important than being home with your children, and you lost out on some of the greatest years of your life. Or maybe you decided finishing a proposal took priority over the monthly report, but the boss came in the next day looking for the report because he needed to present it at a board meeting.

---

[37] George Sweeting, *Great Quotes & Illustrations* (Waco, Texas: Word Books, 1985), pp. 200-201

Most of us have been in situations where we just missed the mark when it came to setting priorities. It's not an uncommon problem. But why do we do it?

1. Lack of focus.

When people don't know exactly what they're working on or what their goals are, they're apt to misprioritize. For example, it's easy for leaders who don't quite know the goals and objectives of the organization to assign meaningless tasks while they search for their focus.

2. Lack of organization.

When people live in worlds of constant disarray and poor planning they never get around to doing the work at hand. Then they rationalize not getting their tasks accomplished because of lack of time. Their disorganization, which is a symptom of poor prioritizing, is the reason they fall short.

3. Fear and misjudgment.

John, the staff officer we talked about earlier, is a perfect example of someone who compromised his priorities because of fear and misjudgment. He had never prioritized before, and he was afraid of the unknown—afraid of giving one assignment precedence over another. So he decided to give everything top priority.

He assumed his subordinates would handle those tasks they felt were more important. Instead, they did the ones that were more appealing, and John's fear and lack of judgment cost him his job.

EMPOWERMENT WORKSHOP

Take a moment and write down three instances when you compromised your priorities. Determine whether it was due to one of the above three reasons. If so, how could you have prevented it?

A Leader's Greatest Enemy

Disorganization is the extraordinary leader's greatest enemy. It's the culprit that can do more damage to a leader's credibility or effectiveness faster than anything else. The longer leaders are disorganized, the less they accomplish and the easier it is for them to lose focus.

Leaders must exhibit an astuteness about planning; they need to focus on long-term results and know what's necessary to obtain those results. In order to invest their best efforts in a particular goal, they need to take charge of their lives and give them direction. Many people don't believe in focusing on a direction. They feel such constraints limit them and their creativity.

Just the opposite is true. People who fail to have direction in their lives limit themselves. They can't get as much accomplished; they waste precious time getting where they want to be, and they often end up going in the wrong direction altogether. I've found personal direction is the best leadership compass I could have as an individual and a leader.

Goal Setting: Taking Charge of Your Life

Goal setting is the only way I know to gain personal direction. It's what helps leaders achieve their inspired visions. Below I've listed eight reasons why it's so important for leaders to set goals.

88

1. Goals give leaders a clear purpose and direction in their lives and help to keep that purpose in perspective.

2. Goals provide leaders the incentive not to procrastinate.

3. Goals are leaders' sources of encouragement.

4. Goals help leaders specify what they want from other people working with them.

5. Goals save leaders time, energy and money.

6. Goals provide a means by which leaders can measure their effectiveness and accomplishments.

7. Goals help leaders focus their concentration.

8. Goals are leaders' foundations for future growth.

Even though goal setting is the best way for leaders to maintain their focus, it's often difficult. Many people fear establishing goals because they don't want reminders that they've failed. But it's important to remember a failure is only a failure if it scares you away from trying new things or attempting to improve yourself.

Achieving goals is a process in which anyone can succeed. People cultivate self-confidence when they complete smaller tasks that contribute to larger ones. Setting realistic, achievable goals provides leaders with a sense of satisfaction and accomplishment. Nothing feels better than being able to scratch off a goal on your list.

But how do you go about setting realistic goals? You don't just pull out a sheet of paper and jot down a list of what you want to accomplish. That's working without direction. When leaders set goals they need to set aims that are definitive and manageable. They must work at setting long-range, intermediate and short-range goals.

Long-Range Goals

These are goals for those objectives you want to accomplish in your lifetime or in 5, 10 or 20 years. They shouldn't be out of sight, just slightly out of reach.

In other words, if it's ludicrous for you to think you can eliminate the homeless problem in your city in one year, you need to readjust your goal to be more realistic. Maybe it's possible for you to reduce the number of homeless people by 50% in five years. If so, set that as a manageable, long-range goal.

Intermediate Goals

These types of goals are short-term breakdowns of long-term goals. They should be aims you can accomplish in the next six months to a year. If your long-range goal is to run a homeless shelter, an intermediate goal would be to visit other shelters in the next few months to see how they started out.

Short-Range Goals

Short-range goals are the stepping stones vital to achieving any major mission in your life. They're easy to work with, bite-sized chunks that help you achieve larger, more long-term goals. To be most effective, they should be broken down into weekly or monthly targets. For example, you may have a short-range goal of raising $500 in one month to purchase blankets for the shelter you want to start.

Whatever you do, when you start setting goals, you must remember to *be specific*. When leaders are establishing their goals, there's no room for ambiguity or timidity. Denis Waitley tells a story in his book, *Seeds Of Greatness*, that reveals how he learned the importance of forming well-defined goals from a 10-year-old child. [38]

Lessons from Eric

Once when Waitley was holding a goal setting workshop, a man brought along his young son, Eric. Waitley thought bringing the child was good positive exposure for the boy and a great opportunity for him to learn more about how the adult world

---

[38] Denis Waitley, *Seeds of Greatness* (Grand Rapids, Michigan: Baker Book House, 1983), pp. 102-105.

operates. Little did he know that he and everyone else in the audience would learn a few things from Eric.

During the seminar, Waitley gave the audience the five questions below to answer about their goals in life:

1. What are your greatest personal and professional abilities and liabilities?

2. What are your most important personal and professional goals for the balance of the year?

3. What is a major personal and professional goal you have for next year?

4. What will your professional level and annual income be in five years?

5. Five years from now:
   Where will you be living?
   What will you be doing?
   What will you have accomplished, that could be written about you by family or peers?
   What state of health will you enjoy?
   What will be your assets in dollars?

The audience was divided into groups and given 40 minutes to work on their answers. Waitley thought it might be fun for Eric to answer the questions for his own life so he gave him his notes from which to copy the questions and a notepad to write his answers.

When Waitley called the small groups back together, he asked them to share their answers aloud. Listing abilities seemed relatively easy to most of the attendees. Waitley received typical answers such as "good with people," "sensitive to the needs of others," and "dedicated." Some of the standard liabilities included "need to organize time and priorities better" and "want to spend more quality time with family."

But when it came to questions two through five, people seemed to have real problems. Question two, concerning personal and professional goals for the balance of the year, received answers such as "to make more, get more, save more

91

and do more." All responses were general and noncommittal. Most people couldn't give a straight answer about their professional levels and incomes. They expected to be making more money, but they wouldn't predict anything because of the uncertainty of the times and inflation. And it was clear that no one could or wanted to pinpoint their future.

That is, no one except Eric. When he volunteered to read his answers, the audience was looking forward to some entertainment, and Waitley figured his responses couldn't be any more ambiguous than those of the others. So he started asking Eric the questions.

"What are your greatest talents and what would you like to improve most?"

"Building model airplanes and scoring high in video computer games are my best things and cleaning my bedroom is what I should do better."

The audience chuckled, but Eric didn't seem concerned.

"What are your personal and professional goals for this year?" said Waitley.

"To complete a model of the Columbia space shuttle craft and earn $450 mowing lawns and shoveling snow."

"What about for next year?" asked Waitley.

"My personal goal is to take a trip to Hawaii, and my professional goal is to earn $700 to pay for the trip."

The impact of Eric's answers was slowly taking effect on both Waitley and the seminar participants. This young boy was speaking about specifics, something none of the adults had been able to do.

"What about your five-year goals?" Waitley continued.

"I'll be 15 and in the 10th grade. I plan to take computer courses and science classes. I should be earning at least $200 a month at a part-time job."

"And in 20 years?"

"I'll be 30 years old, living in Houston, Texas, or Cape Canaveral, Florida. I'll be a space shuttle astronaut working for NASA or a big company. I will have put new TV satellites into orbit, and I'll be delivering parts for a new launching station in space. I'll also be in good physical shape because you have to be in good shape to be an astronaut."

The audience wasn't laughing anymore. A 10-year-old had shown that they had just spent 40 minutes talking in circles with themselves and each other.

Eric had shown everyone the whole key to setting goals was specificity. Most 10-year-olds believe they can achieve their dreams no matter what they are, and that's part of the beauty of youth. The beauty of leadership is the same. Eric's innocence and naiveté had removed the constraints that would have hindered his responses, and it's a great lesson for all of us to learn.

Maintaining Perspective

I believe we should all look at goal setting from a child's point of view. We should view it without fear of rejection, failure or ridicule. If, as adults, we continued to believe in ourselves the way we did as children, we probably wouldn't have so much trouble with leadership.

We do, however, have to maintain our perspective when we set goals. To do that, our goals should be reviewed often and updated. We may discover as we're trying to achieve them that they were a little too far out of our reach. That doesn't mean we have to give them up altogether; it just means readjusting them.

One of the best ways I've discovered for monitoring my goals is to keep a chart of my progress. It doesn't have to be anything fancy—just a sheet where I can record those tasks I've completed and the dates they were finished. This not only helps me see my accomplishments, but it also shows me where I may have misjudged the amount of time I thought was necessary for a particular project.

By charting my progress I also create a visual aid that shows me when I may need to reevaluate my objectives. I may discover that, although attainable, some of my goals are misprioritized. The progress chart allows me to see how I can work with them and make adjustments to better fit my needs.

93

The Leader's Most Precious Asset

As far as I'm concerned, time is the leader's greatest treasure. In today's fast-paced world, business people often equate time with money. So, obviously, it's a commodity worth investing in.

It's true that no matter what we do we can't control time; however, time can control us. Poor time management is a common organizational problem among leaders. People often unconsciously let their guard down just enough that time-wasting habits edge in to their lives and begin to rob them of their energy, money and effectiveness.

But there is hope. If you haven't already taken steps to improve your time management, let me assure you it can be done. It starts with three basic principles:

1. *Learn to control your habits.*

We all have habits, some good and some bad. The key is to focus on the good and eliminate the bad. But maybe you don't think you have time-wasting habits. How can you determine whether you do? Analyze your time-robbers.

For example, keep a log of *everything* you do for one week. If you spend five minutes on hold when you call the bank about their loan policy, write it down. If you take a 15-minute coffee break, be sure to record it as well. You will be shocked to discover how little of your day is actually spent doing productive work.

Once you see where you consistently waste time, you can work on eliminating those habits. Maybe you shouldn't take your break at the same time everyone else does because you tend to socialize longer than necessary. Good leaders do whatever is necessary to protect their time.

I've also discovered that maintaining a personal and professional schedule can eliminate a great deal of these problems. If you have a schedule you can constantly refer to, you're less apt to let distractions intervene with your plans. Having a strategy for each day and week is a great way to discipline yourself.

94

I make it a habit to start and finish my days and weeks with a plan. Everyday, before I leave the office, I write down what I want to accomplish during the next day. I prioritize my tasks so when I come to work in the morning I don't have to waste any time getting my thoughts together and planning my day. It's already done, and I can immediately get to work.

2. *Learn to avoid distractions.*

The three most common distractions are socializing, paper shuffling and interruptions.

Socializing

We briefly touched on socializing when we talked about taking breaks at different times. Excessive socializing is a major timewaster, and it should be eliminated.

I've found if I limit my socializing to before work hours or immediately after them, I can control my time much better. I'm not saying you should take a vow of silence and not carry on conversations with other people, because all healthy work environments need to have some social interaction. But you shouldn't allow socializing to become such a consistent habit that it interferes with your production.

Leaders are often the ones people will seek out to talk to when they have a problem. Extraordinary leaders learn the value of *tactfully* redirecting conversations to a more convenient time. Some leaders I know schedule mini-conferences and lunches with people so problem-airing or socializing can occur then.

Paper Shuffling

Leaders also need to safeguard themselves from getting caught in the paper shuffle. Have you ever found yourself going through piles of papers on your desk only to create different piles and never do anything about them? I really struggled with this until I decided I wasn't going to allow myself to become a chronic shuffler.

Now, when the mail comes or I have a stack of paperwork on my desk, I go through it *once*. I file what needs to be filed. I throw away everything that's unnecessary. And I complete work on what needs immediate attention.

Interruptions

The third way to help yourself eliminate distractions is learn to manage your interruptions. The telephone and those who work for you are the two main causes of interruptions. To reduce them, I suggest establishing a phone policy and an open-door policy.

Establish certain hours when you will accept phone calls and certain ones when you will make them. Pretty soon people calling you will get the idea that if they want to catch you the first time they should call during the hours you accept calls. And by setting a call-out hour you prevent yourself from being distracted by important calls that need to be made.

To control drop-in associates, designate open-door office hours. I firmly believe in the open-door policy for leaders. People should know they can approach you with their concerns and ideas. But it's unrealistic for others to have access to you all day. Your work would be continually interrupted.

College professors are known for setting office hours, and it's a concept that could work for every type of leader. Let people know you welcome them coming to you but *only* during the hour or two you designate as open-door. They will find you approachable, but they will also learn to value your work time.

3. *Learn to identify why you procrastinate.*

Procrastination is the most cunning time-robber of all, and leaders need to know when they do it and how they can capture it before it captures them. But why do we procrastinate? What makes us so vulnerable to putting tasks off?

Habit

People can't break their old habits. So many of us continue to do things the way we always have whether or not its conducive to good time management. For example, what route do you take to work every morning? Do you go that way because it's the most direct way to your office or do you just do it out of habit?

Poor Planning

We discussed this at length earlier. The main point to remember is: Leaders who don't have a written plan they can follow every day waste time. They start to act on whim or judgment and forget about prioritizing altogether.

Underestimating a Task

Often, people fail to take everything into consideration when they tackle a project. They underestimate it.

Not long ago, one of my friends, a leader in a social club, was in charge of finding a building in which they could meet. They had been meeting in a fire hall. But they received the opportunity to purchase an old church fellowship hall and renovate it to fit their needs.

My friend estimated it would take $2,500 and two to three weeks to do the necessary changes. But he had greatly underestimated both the cost and time. As he organized the project he became aware of his error.

He started backing away from his proposed schedule and blaming the delay on several "unforeseen circumstances." Once he realized he didn't have enough time, manpower or money to complete the renovation, he wanted to "save face," so he started procrastinating.

As a result, my friend lost his credibility as well as his leadership position. The club had to initiate a huge fund-raising drive to make up for his error and hire a construction team to finish the work.

Fear or Dread

People fear the unknown, and they dread the disagreeable. When we don't like to do something or we don't know how to do it, we can come up with hundreds of excuses for putting it off. Through my leadership seminars, I've talked with several people who feared venturing into leadership roles. As a result they procrastinated. They put off making final decisions or following through on their responsibilities. Of course, we all know the longer we put something off the worse it gets.

Catching the Thief

Eliminating procrastination isn't always easy. It means confronting those issues that make us uncomfortable and admitting we have a problem. Most people like to believe procrastination is a symptom of laziness. But it usually isn't. Rather, it's the result of being in a rut of living with poor habits.

We all suffer from procrastination at one time or another. Leaders are no exception. Remember, you're not weak for struggling with procrastination. What makes a person weak is failing to correct the problem. So before I close this chapter, I'd like to provide you with five steps that have helped me learn to beat procrastination in my life.

1. Learn to schedule your life properly.

Living by a schedule doesn't hinder your life, creativity or spontaneity. There's always room for spontaneity. However, if you're serious about becoming an extraordinary leader, you will schedule your life so you can get the most done in the least amount of time.

If you don't have a calendar you can carry with you to keep track of your appointments and tasks, go out and get one today. It will be the wisest investment you will ever make to help cultivate your leadership effectiveness.

2. *Be self-disciplined.*

Extraordinary leaders take control of their lives. They realize how much the effect of their self-discipline relates to their credibility. They exhibit self-discipline in their appearances as well as their personal and professional lives.

3. *Maintain a list of tasks with target dates or times for completion.*

This relates to goal setting. It's a proven fact that scheduling tasks helps people manage their time. A schedule provides a great means of guidance and encouragement. Effective leaders pre-plan their tasks in detail so they avoid underestimating the work. They also regularly reevaluate their goals and progress to assure they're remaining on track.

4. *When possible, share unpleasant tasks.*

Since it's so easy to procrastinate when you're faced with something unpleasant, try finding someone to share the job with. It's a lot easier to take on a disagreeable project when two people tackle it than when one faces it alone. The task doesn't become so overwhelming, and the job goes by more quickly.

5. *Be decisive.*

Determined leaders know not to procrastinate when it comes to making decisions. The best policy is to *act.* Don't wait for decisions to become easier or for someone else to make them. You could be waiting a long time. Extraordinary leaders gather all the facts they need and make decisions as quickly as possible.

Decisiveness is the mark of confident leadership, and confident leaders make extraordinary leaders. If you struggle with making decisions, take heart. You can empower yourself to become a better decision-maker. In the next chapter we will focus on exactly how you can master that art.

6

EMPOWERMENT PRINCIPLE #5
Leaders Realize the Impact of Being Decisive

"A man with a half volition goes backwards and forwards, and makes no way on the smoothest road; a man with a whole volition advances on the roughest, and will reach his purpose, if there be even a little worthiness in it. The man without a purpose is like a ship without a rudder—a waif, a nothing, a no man."

—*Thomas Carlyle* [39]

---

[39] George Sweeting, *Great Quotes & Illustrations* (Waco, Texas: Word Books, 1985), p. 83.

Mobilizing Yourself for Action

Decision making is what moves leaders backwards from or forwards toward their inspired visions. It's often what reveals the differences between the mediocre and the exceptional leader. As a result, many people fear making decisions more than any other aspect of the leadership role.

I don't blame people for being afraid. Leaders often face severe repercussions from their choices—ridicule, impeachment, or prison. Consider the outcome of some of our well-known leaders' decisions and how their choices reflected their leadership capabilities—the Iran-contra affair, the invasion of Panama, telephone deregulation, the sale of Eastern Airlines, and even the purchase of an air-conditioned dog house.

Most people, especially those in leadership positions, don't enjoy being unpopular or disliked. They need the emotional support of others. Therefore, it's not uncommon for people to avoid making decisions to escape potential problems.

Extraordinary leaders, however, rise above this fear. They recognize making an unpopular decision is almost always better than losing respect and credibility from making no decision. They learn how to confront their fears and recognize the reasons they avoid decision making. Then they work to overcome them.

I'm sure a tired, old black woman named Rosa Parks feared what her decision not to give up her seat on a bus to a white man would do. And I wouldn't doubt Captain Lawrence C. Chambers agonized over his decision whether or not to push helicopters over the side of the *USS Midway* to let a tiny plane carrying a South Vietnamese officer and his family land. These

103

leaders knew how important it was for them not to dodge their decisions or let fear get the best of them.

Empowerment Principle #5:
Extraordinary leaders understand sound decision making impacts their leadership credibility and balances them on the fine line between success and failure.

I've discovered eight common ways we tend to avoid making decisions. At some point in my life, I've experienced all of them; most likely you have too.

The Big Eight

Procrastination

In the previous chapter we discussed how easily this thief can rob us of our time. But procrastination doesn't just steal our time; it also carries away our confidence. Have you ever noticed the longer you delay making an important decision, the less confident you become? Postponing decisions causes people to question their judgment. Eventually, it allows doubt to crowd into their thoughts, and they become paralyzed by fear.

Procrastinating leaders are easily recognizable. They take weeks deciding something that could have been decided in a few days. They try to reassure themselves they're making the right choice by putting off action until the last possible moment. Or they have a hundred excuses why they don't have time to address the issue.

Ineffective Delegation

Many leaders don't know how to effectively delegate tasks and responsibilities. Because of this inability, they're burdened with even more responsibility than is necessary for their roles.

Leaders who do this insulate themselves from the responsibility of making decisions. They enfold themselves in a protective covering of overwork. That way, they can rationalize having little time for decision making. You will often hear how these leaders push aside issues requiring action. They're just "too busy" to deal with them.

The leader of a civic organization I used to be involved in used this excuse repeatedly. Every time I went to him for his decision on a program or change I was instituting, he had some other top priority work to do before he could look at it. I always heard how his "back was against the wall."

Needless to say, we never got anything accomplished in that organization. And eventually the leader resigned from his position because of stress and fatigue.

Policy Harping

Leaders who are rigid about following policy often cannot make their own decisions. They rely so heavily "on the book" they don't cultivate their own decision making skills. Whatever the book says is what they do. No more, no less.

People who have fallen into the policy harping trap usually fear deviating from standard procedure for several reasons. They don't want to be held accountable for poor decisions, so rules become their scapegoats. They want to avoid struggling over serious problems and making unpopular choices, so regulations become crutches.

Don't get me wrong. Policies can be vital. They often control production and safety. But when leaders use rules and regulations to avoid making their own decisions, problems arise.

I met a woman at one of my leadership seminars who worked for a cabinet manufacturer. She was a line supervisor and was interested in increasing production for her division as well as the company. She noticed many line workers were getting cramps in their hands from the repetitive motions they performed day after day.

To abate the problem, she went to the production supervisor requesting they rotate the workers on different jobs and provide more breaks so they could rest their hands. She believed this would not only help people work better, but also decrease the number of absences due to injured hands.

The supervisor pulled out the company handbook and told her the guidelines stated workers were to be trained in *one* area, and they were allotted only *two* 15-minute breaks per day. They were not about to deviate from policy.

The truth was he knew the assembly workers needed exactly what the line supervisor was suggesting, but he was afraid to make a decision or suggest changes that might bring down the wrath of upper management. As a result, his section of the manufacturing process continued to produce fewer and fewer cabinet parts, hindering the entire production line.

Eventually, the workers went on strike because of the poor working conditions. Had the production supervisor been willing to make decisions and suggest changes to company policy, he might never have had to deal with the strike.

Passing the Buck

Some leaders are chronic buck passers. They're people who can't rely on their own judgment. They find ways to sidestep responsibility. They're also the ones who, if they can't find the solution in the company handbook, pass it on to someone who supposedly has the authority to deal with it.

For years, buck-passing has resulted in more problems than almost anything else in organizations. I know of a railroad company that suffered so much from this problem they lost millions of dollars.

When a problem was discovered by the vice presidents, they would pass on their responsibility of handling it to their assistants. The assistants would then pass it on to the division managers, and the managers would send it to the supervisors. Inevitably, somewhere along the line the problem became distorted and the solution ignored.

It wasn't until after they reorganized that the company realized people were continually passing decisions around until they were conveniently forgotten. By that point, they had lost more than two million dollars due to unresolved problems.

Double Talk

Leaders who avoid making decisions through double talk water down their answers. They skirt the real issues because they don't want to risk offending or upsetting anyone. Ultimately, their double talk causes confusion and misdirection.

For example, a project manager named Bill was in charge of reading, editing and approving proposals for future projects. Even if a proposal was unacceptable, he was so afraid of hurting a staff member's feelings or discouraging him or her that he engaged in double talk.

When Bill discussed an inadequate proposal with a staff member, he diminished its problems to avoid making the staffer feel like a failure and to avoid conflict. Unconsciously, he was playing a mind game.

Instead of helping to improve the quality of the proposals, Bill was contributing to the problem. In order to be effective, he needed to decide immediately whether a proposal was acceptable and discuss the matter with the appropriate person in a straightforward manner. His current method of double talk was leaving staffers confused and often falsely encouraged.

Initiating a Study to Determine All Facts

This is a common method of procrastination used by insecure leaders who refuse to make decisions. These people want to review every angle of a problem and be sure they have all the facts in front of them before taking any action. It's rare, of course, that all facts are available.

And these procrastinators know that. Therefore, the decision gets placed on the back burner for an indefinite amount of time, or the process of acquiring the information takes so long the opportunity to act slips by.

Seeking Counsel from Experts

Chronic worriers and shy, timid leaders use this avoidance technique most often. These leaders have such little self-confidence they seek advice from everyone—including people whose opinions are irrelevant in the situation—before they will risk making a move. Their lack of courage allows them to continue fooling themselves into believing they're actually working on making a decision.

I've had several people, especially in the college setting, come to me for advice on a particular decision that had nothing to do with me. These people were merely seeking agreement, so they wouldn't feel bad if the results of their decisions were less than they hoped they would be.

Evading

Leaders who evade don't initially appear to be people who avoid making decisions because they go through all the necessary steps to *look* like they're doing something about the situation. In reality, they're crippled by fear or lack of confidence.

When you ask about its status, they say they're "working on it." But they've actually done nothing about the situation. When the heat is on, they conveniently push the decision aside and give something else priority over it.

The Fate of an Indecisive Leader

Philosopher-psychologist William James once said, "There is no more miserable human being than one in whom nothing is habitual but indecision." [40] I believe him. The main reason indecisive people are so miserable is they are unstable in all they do. They are double-minded.

When leaders are double-minded, they allow weeds to grow in the soil of opportunity. One of the most obvious results of this attitude is unwillingness to take risks. Indecision usually manifests itself in two ways:

---

[40] Ibid, p. 82.

Lost Opportunity

When leaders put off making decisions long enough or fail to make them at all, they pass up many opportunities. Not only do they cause themselves or their organizations to lose money, but they may also miss a once-in-a-lifetime chance for achieving their goals or capturing their visions.

Risky decisions are the ones most avoided, yet they're often the ones most lucrative if followed through. There's nothing worse than a feeling of regret, and indecisive leaders live in its shadow. A wavering attitude can often mean the difference in a mediocre leader and a great leader.

Loss of Respect

In most situations, if the leader misses an opportunity to make a decision on something, he or she is likely to lose respect from others. No one likes to follow leaders who can't make up their minds. I can remember as a teenager having a friend who could never decide what he wanted to do.

Nothing frustrated me more than Friday nights with this friend. I couldn't understand what was so hard about deciding whether to go to the movies or the soda shop.

The same thing can happen with leaders. If you're a person who can't make up his or her mind whether to eat the chicken or the fish at dinner, you're going to lose some respect. I can guarantee you will lose even more if you can't make a sound decision when it comes to something serious in your leadership role.

For example, a leader who can't decide how to reprimand a disruptive person, because he or she is afraid of hurting the person's feelings, reveals a lot of cowardice and self-doubt. And no one likes to put their trust and respect in a person like that.

The Formula for Success

In extraordinary leadership, the formula for success is: decide and act. But people are not born decision-makers. As a matter of fact, each one of us had to go through a learning process as we were growing up to discover how to make responsible decisions. It took a lot of cultivating and modeling by our parents and teachers to help us acquire the necessary skills for sound decision making. Unfortunately, many of us as adults *still* haven't mastered this skill.

People are often shocked to realize when they acquire leadership status they don't instantly know how to make the most productive decisions. They become disillusioned because making decisions as a leader is not like making decisions for themselves. So much more is involved.

We all fail to make the right choices at times. For people who wish to become extraordinary leaders, this is a constant reality. You're not always going to know what to do. You're going to make mistakes. But as author and philosopher Wilfred A. Peterson says, "Decision is the courageous facing of issues, knowing that if they are not faced, problems will remain forever unanswered." [41] The best way to courageously face decision making is to discover what is the best strategy for you. I guarantee you will decrease your chances of failure significantly by learning how best to approach decision making.

Below is a strategy that works well. Since this plan has a proven track record for me and many others, it may be worth your consideration.

1. Be discerning.

Having a sharp outlook is a skill that will help you prevent crises. Extraordinary leaders know how to be sensitive, alert and perceptive. They spot problems before they arise or get blown out of proportion.

To do this, you need to become a regular observer. Always check out what appears to be an insignificant symptom. If the opportunity arises to correct a problem in its earliest stages, you will save yourself and others unnecessary grief and possibly some harder decisions down the road.

---

[41] As quoted by Sheila Murray Bethel, *Making A Difference: Twelve Qualities That Make You A Leader* (New York: G.P. Putnam's Sons, 1990), p. 149.

```
EMPOWERMENT WORKSHOP
```

When in the past could you have been more discerning or alert to potential problems and have made your decision making easier?

2. Keep communication lines open.

Clear, open communication lines are a leader's access to future problems and potential opportunities. When there's a free exchange among leaders and followers, leaders invite people to share information with them. Once you've fostered this kind of environment, you will be able to discern when problems are in the making.

For example, an unusual break in communication with one employee could signal a problem. And when there's a situation that requires a decision, open communication will help you clarify the situation, keep things under control and discover a satisfactory solution.

3. Clearly diagnose and define the problem.

Failure to clearly define problems is probably the most common reason people fall into the trap of indecision. No one can solve a problem without first knowing exactly what it is. In other words, leaders have to look beyond the symptoms and locate the actual problem.

Let's say your car didn't start this morning. What do you think the problem is? It's making a kind of choking sound so you think it may be the carburetor. You check it, but you find nothing wrong. You check to make sure you have gas; you have plenty. Now you're baffled. You don't know what to do so you call to have the car towed to the garage.

111

You were only treating the symptoms of your car problem—based on the sounds you heard and the way it acted. Had you taken the time to determine why that noise was occurring and what could have been causing it, you would have discovered there was only a kink in the fuel line, preventing gas from reaching the engine.

By determining where the problem lies, you save time and money in the long run. So learn to diagnose and state problems specifically.

4. Gather the facts and analyze the problem.

Once you've defined a problem, it's important to gather all available facts. By clearly and concisely defining it, you will know exactly what information you will need to make a decision. Remember, don't waste time waiting for information that's not available or hedge making a decision because you don't have enough facts.

Use the information you can get that doesn't cause too much delay or expense. When you've collected as many of the facts as you can, analyze the problem. Make sure you do your homework so you can correctly identify the problem in the first place and review the situation.

5. List all possible options.

In most cases, there's more than one solution to a problem. An effective leader learns to explore all options to determine which is the best one. The key to doing this is maintaining flexibility and an open mind.

Don't always follow your tendencies to handle a problem or make a decision based on the way you normally handle situations. Even though habit can be comfortable, it can also be a hindrance. Don't limit yourself with your prejudices. Personal preferences can hinder you from looking at other, possibly better, solutions.

6. *Select the best solution and act on it.*

The hardest part of decision making is taking the time to consider all options and selecting the best one. To do this, leaders need to look at the pros and cons of each possibility. What positive aspects will help you solve the problem? What negative ones will hinder its solution?

One of the best ways I've found to do this is to visualize the outcome of each option. In other words, I try to foresee the consequences. Then I choose the solution with the most positive effects and the least number of negative ones. I realize this can still be a risk, but extraordinary leaders are willing to take risks to see things get accomplished.

Effective leaders act on their decisions. Verbally deciding is not enough. They decide *how* the solution will be implemented, *who* will help do it and *when* it will be accomplished. You need to have a well thought-out plan for instituting your decision that covers all areas. If you're serious about leadership, you need to act in a way that assures results.

7. *Inform those people affected by the decision.*

Most likely the decisions you make are going to involve people other than yourself. Extraordinary leaders realize the value in involving those who will be affected by the outcome in the decision making process.

If it's not feasible to include them, leaders immediately inform those people of the decision. Nothing is worse than hearing through the grapevine about a major decision or change in the organization that involves you. By informing everyone throughout the process, you will gain support and guarantee your decision is carried out.

8. *Follow up on your decision.*

Never assume once you've made a decision that all is well. Anything can go wrong at any time. By following up you assure yourself and the organization that what needs to be implemented is implemented.

113

I'm not saying you should be concerned with every detail of the process. But you shouldn't just make a decision and leave those responsible for carrying it out alone to handle it. By routinely checking the progress of your solution, you will not only confirm that everything is going according to plan, but you will also have the opportunity to foresee any potential problems.

The railroad company I mentioned earlier made the mistake of not following up. The vice presidents assumed their assistants would take care of the problem. The same was true of everyone along the buck passing path. As a result, the consequences of failing to check progress cost the company a great deal of money.

9. Assess the results of the decision.

Once your decision has been implemented, evaluate the results. Did you achieve what you intended? What kinds of problems did you run across? Each decision making process should be a learning experience. By examining your successes and your failures, you can learn a great deal about how to handle future decisions and improve your leadership ability.

Decision Making at Its Best

I won't say that decision making is easy because it's not. It's often quite difficult. But if you're serious about breaking out of the ordinary to make a difference, you have to break out of old habits that hinder effective decision making and focus on obtaining results. To close this chapter, I'd like to offer you five decision making tips I've found most helpful:

1. Frame the decision.

We talked about framing in Chapter 2. When you're going to frame a picture for your home, you usually try several different styles before you decide which one accentuates the artwork the way you want.

The framing process in decision making is similar. Leaders should visualize a frame around their decisions to determine which one emphasizes the most productive outcome.

2. *Make timely, yet unrushed decisions.*

Extraordinary leaders need to learn how to manage their decision making time. In other words, they shouldn't waste excessive time on little decisions or rush through critical ones. When petty problems take attention away from the more serious concerns that need total concentration, leaders lose their abilities to discern levels of significance and make sound choices.

Most of us tend to focus more time and energy on larger, more difficult situations. But this can create serious problems when the decision gets drawn out longer and longer. Effective leaders find the delicate balance between critical and less important issues. They learn to manage themselves so they can make the most productive choices in an appropriate time span. They know the value of deadlines.

3. *Seek appropriate advice.*

"Careless living will always create doubt, but the opposite is also true. Doubt leads to careless living." [42] Leaders need to be willing to take risks, but they certainly don't have to risk being in doubt or making a decision with which they're uncomfortable.

Never become so wrapped up in your decisions that you can't seek the advice of others. When you're in doubt, seek people who are informed on the subject you're dealing with. If you're deciding how to initiate a new task force into your company without unsettling the other employees and you've never done this before, you'd be foolish not to try and find someone who could advise you.

Consultation with someone else during decision making is important for fostering quality relationships. Asking for

---

[42] Sweeting, *Great Quotes,* p. 98.

115

help puts leaders in the position of recognizing they aren't the ones with all the answers. People respect that.

Most people even prefer working with someone who knows they aren't right all of the time and may need help in areas where they fall short. Everyone has weaknesses, but the leader who fails to ask for advice when in a tough decision making situation exhibits the ultimate weakness.

4. *Trust your intuition.*

All leaders face crises at some point or another. It comes with the territory. Even though you may be forced to make quick decisions in a crisis, you should never ignore your instincts. A leader's intuition can be his or her greatest asset.

Many times in emergency situations people are forced to make swift decisions without proper information; they have to rely on their intuition. Most of the time their reactions are right.

I'm not saying you should follow your instincts all the time because that's absurd. You'd become biased, and you would lose sight of practical, more informed reasons for making particular choices. However, wise leaders recognize when their hunches are telling them something critical about a certain decision.

5. *Don't worry over past decisions.*

When you've made a decision be sure to evaluate the results of it, but under no circumstance should you worry over it. Human beings fail. They miss the mark many times. And no leader is exempt from this reality. Even famous leaders have made poor decisions.

President Kennedy certainly wasn't popular for his Bay of Pigs decision. The "coup" attempt on Fidel Castro resulted in a slaughter. However, Kennedy didn't brood over his poor choice and allow it to immobilize him. He learned from it.

When the Cuban Missile Crisis emerged, he could have let his past decision influence him not to take action. But he didn't. He confronted Nikita Khrushchev and Castro about

116

their military alliance and assured that Soviet missiles were removed from Cuba. This time his decision was a success.

The key is not to worry about the past. Lay it to rest, but learn from the mistakes you made. Think of worry this way:

"Worry is a thin stream of fear trickling through the mind. If encouraged, it cuts a channel into which all other thoughts are drained." [43]

Extraordinary leaders don't allow that trickle to enter their minds, and they don't allow themselves to get ulcers. They know they can't do much to change the past, but they sure can learn to do better in the future.

Since there's no way to avoid making decisions, wise leaders learn how to cope with the process. They confront their fears about decision making and show their leadership finesse by remaining consistent, reliable and wise when they make choices.

As you will discover in the next chapter, consistency, reliability and wisdom mean a lot to the extraordinary leader; they're the attributes of an ethical leader. And without a strong sense of ethics, leaders are nothing.

[43] Ibid, p, 268.

7

EMPOWERMENT PRINCIPLE #6
Leaders Have High Ethical Standards

"The prosperity of a country depends not on the abundance of its revenues, nor on the strength of its fortifications, nor on the beauty of its public buildings, but it consists in the number of its men of enlightenment and character."

—*Martin Luther* [44]

"All human beings are endowed with a moral sense."

—*Thomas Jefferson* [45]

---

[44] Eleanor Doan, *The New Speaker's Sourcebook* (Grand Rapids, Michigan: Zondervan Publishing House, 1968), p. 135.
[45] As quoted by Sheila Murray Bethel, *Making a Difference* (New York: G.P. Putnam's Sons, 1990), p. 63.

The Pinnacle of Leadership

A sense of rightness resides deep inside us all. We each believe in a set of principles—what is proper or improper. The way we behave, reach decisions and live reflects those standards. We cannot escape the way our ethics affect our lives. They not only direct the way we act, but also the way others act toward us. A person's ethics are the criteria by which people judge leaders as worthy of their jobs.

Most of us want political leaders who won't lie to us, business leaders who won't take unfair advantage of us and school officials who won't hurt our children. We want leaders with high ethics.

The truth is: High ethical standards are the guiding force behind an extraordinary leader's decisions and actions. Because leaders are the ones most often in public view, they're the ones most critically affected by this truth. The more strict we are with upholding ethical behavior, the better leaders we will become.

Empowerment Principle #6:
Extraordinary leaders maintain a level of integrity and ethical behavior that sets them apart from the ordinary.

What Are Ethics?

When we talk about ethics, we're referring to the standards or judgments of personal responsibility we place on ourselves.

They're the convictions under which we live our lives—those inner proddings that influence us to act in a particular manner.

Our ethics encompass our moral codes of conduct, the principles or individual "laws" that determine our views of good and bad, right and wrong. Our ethics are by-products of what we believe to be morally sound; they direct the way we behave in any given situation.

For example, you might believe it's improper for you, as a leader, to socialize away from work with subordinates of the opposite sex. Your moral code establishes infidelity as wrong, and you view this type of socializing as a form of infidelity. Your ethical standards, then, would define this as unacceptable behavior, and you would refuse to participate in it.

Leaders need to establish ethical standards concerning all aspects of their leadership roles. What's important to remember is those ethics make the difference in your perception as an effective leader.

Personal Ethics Versus Perceived Ethics

Ethical standards are critical to a person's credibility. People constantly watch their leaders out of the corners of their eyes. They want to ensure they're not following a deceitful person. Extraordinary leaders recognize this. They know the personal and professional impact of living with clear, unyielding principles, and they work hard to incorporate into their lives principles such as:

Honesty

Respect for others

Integrity

Fairness

Kindness

Decency

Ethics fall into two categories: personal and perceived. Effective leaders need to understand the difference between the two and learn how to balance both areas for maximum credibility.

Personal Ethics

These ethical standards are those which leaders feel are proper behavior in their personal lives as well as in the organizations they're a part of. For example, they're the standards by which you ask yourself whether you're going to allow the fellows at the lodge to make sexual innuendos about your neighbor's wife. Are you going to let it slip by that an associate fudged on his or her expense reports? Or is it acceptable to allow employees to take advantage of comp time even though company policy prohibits it?

A leader's personal and professional ethics need to be congruent. In other words, if you believe it's wrong to cheat, and at home you teach your child this principle, you're not maintaining your personal ethics by falsifying your expense report at work the next day.

Perceived Ethics

Perceived ethics are those which others see in you, regardless of your intentions. Perceived ethics determine to what extent people are willing to commit to your leadership.

Even though you may have high principles for yourself and may know where you stand in certain situations, the way others perceive your actions has everything to do with your credibility in their eyes.

For example, personally you may find nothing wrong with eating lunch with a subordinate of the opposite sex. In your eyes and your lunch partner's, it's an innocent act. However, others in your office may *perceive* this action as a form of favoritism, which could undermine your authority with them. Or, regardless of your intentions, they could also perceive it as more than an innocent, social luncheon and assume you're having an affair with the person.

123

Because others' perceptions can cause problems, extraordinary leaders need to adjust their actions to assure they reflect the highest standards possible. For instance, you may have to decline the one-on-one luncheons with subordinates of the opposite sex.

Leaders need to realize their perceived ethics should be on a higher level than their personal ones. Consider this example. A member of Congress may have high personal ethics and stress that no favors or gifts could ever sway him or her to vote a particular way. Because this person has such high principles regarding this issue, he or she may see nothing wrong with accepting a cruise at the expense of an influential lobbyist. After all, the gift has nothing to do with the vote, right?

Would *you* believe that cruise didn't sway his or her vote? Most likely not. Even though the congressperson's morals strictly prohibit such unprincipled action, our perception of the situation suggests otherwise.

Forging Your Working Tenets

Because of perceptions, leaders have a personal responsibility to behave properly and set examples for others. Since a person's life, actions and behavior influence others, we each must be held accountable for the impact we make.

Certainly, leaders must *live by* the ethical standards they expect of others. If they don't, they have no right to retain their positions. It's a proven fact that leaders' ethics have an impact on an organization and other people. Consider how former television evangelist Jim Bakker's ethics affected others. His fraudulent, unscrupulous behavior had an impact not only on himself and his family, but also on the United States government, Christian organizations nationwide and those individuals who had emotionally, spiritually and financially supported his mission.

Ethical standards are vital to the way the public views leadership. Where ethics are concerned, leaders have great responsibility.

124

1. Leaders must clarify and express ethical behavior both verbally and by example.

John Ackers, chairman of IBM, once said, " . . . common moral sense doesn't come out of nowhere. We must consciously and vigorously work at fortifying our ethical buttresses." [46] In other words, if you want to make a difference, you have to set a constructive example for others. It's up to you to establish the level of conduct you believe is appropriate for yourself, your family and the organizations you're involved in.

When leaders communicate their standards by establishing and following a set of rules, they set a precedent for others. If you want people to respond positively to your leadership, you must ensure that your standards of behavior are clear and concise.

2. Leaders must create an ethical premise that everyone understands and expects.

Ethical standards are hard to define because there's no exact formula for creating them, and people differ in their views of right and wrong. Regardless of the difficulty in determining absolute rights and wrongs, you have a responsibility for guaranteeing that others know where you draw the line. Remember this one statement: No one should *ever* have to wonder where you or the organization stands when it comes to questionable behavior.

As a leader you have the right to determine what your ethical absolutes are. If you think it's wrong to use the copy machine at the Red Cross headquarters for personal use, then you can establish a rule about it and scrupulously observe the mandate. Other people may not agree with you, but in the long run they will respect you for sticking to your standards. You will also facilitate a strong bond of trust and cooperation.

---

[46] Ibid, p. 63.

3. Leaders must immediately handle any ethical problems that develop.

Effective leaders know that once an ethical premise is set, it must be followed. If you have publicly established your standards and your behavior reflects them, you must never fail to institute the consequences of deviating from them. People see leaders who are inconsistent about enforcing ethical standards as unprofessional and hypocritical.

Subordinates depend on their leaders to initiate discipline. When leaders act swiftly and consistently to enforce all standards, they earn a high level of respect.

The Problem with Desensitization

Have you ever been around a person who was indifferent to unethical behavior? I've had the unfortunate experience of being around several people who seemed unconcerned when they or others in their organizations were involved in questionable practices. I've also seen people who simply didn't have the courage to stand up against inappropriate behavior. I call this desensitization.

For example, baseball manager Billy Martin said cheating was as much a part of baseball as hot dogs and scorecards. [47] It had been going on for years, and Martin was one of many who had become desensitized to it. He didn't view cheating as cheating because everyone did it.

Instead, it was a way to get any edge he could. And no one, especially Martin, wanted to be at a disadvantage. So he allowed throws like spitters and sinkers, where his pitchers applied substances to or somehow roughed up the ball. Eventually, his "advantage" grew to include even more dishonest practices.

Once when Martin managed the Oakland A's, he got thrown out of a game. He went to his office turned on the television and got an open line to the dugout. He proceeded

---

[47] Billy Martin with Phil Pepe, *Billyball* (Garden City, New York: Doubleday & Co., Inc., 1987), pp. 157-159.

to manage the game from there until the owner, Roy Eisenhardt came in. Eisenhardt told Martin to stop because it was wrong. Martin acted like he conceded and hung up the phone. But when the owner left, Martin dressed in street clothes and went to the bar of a nearby Holiday Inn. Of course the game was on, and he got another open line to manage the game from there.

Martin's actions were unethical. He was thoroughly desensitized, so he rationalized everything he did. If you intend to be an extraordinary leader you cannot risk becoming desensitized to unethical behavior.

Unprincipled behavior doesn't exist only in baseball; it's all around us. We can't allow ourselves to remain silent about it. Silence in the face of corruption demoralizes us. It demoralizes our organizations, the people who work with us and, ultimately, our country.

The Key to Credibility

Leaders carry their credibility and integrity in the same pocket as their ethics. If a magician says he's going to pull a rabbit out of a hat, and he pulls out a scarf, that doesn't do much for his credibility. The same is true for leaders. Washington, D.C.'s Mayor, Marion Barry, certainly lost his credibility as an anti-drug campaigner, as mayor and as a person when he was arrested for cocaine possession. And Jim Bakker lost his integrity as a minister of the Gospel since he so blatantly ignored its teachings.

Living ethically is not easy; it requires courage and perseverance. It takes a committed person to stand up to injustice or corruption. But it's vital that leaders cultivate this strength of character so they can make a difference.

The story of Janie Forsythe provides an example of a young girl who had the courage to stand up against what she thought was unjust. Her actions made her an extraordinary leader.

In Anniston, Alabama, on May 4, 1961, thirteen black "Freedom Riders" were on a bus which a group of angry

127

whites forced off the road. The attackers tried to get on the bus to beat the riders, but the doors were locked. They set fire to the bus and waited for the riders to scramble off. When the blacks did succumb to the smoke, the mob beat and kicked them until they, too, had to move back because of the smoke.

When twelve-year-old Janie saw what was happening outside her house she became angry. She couldn't believe the mob was watching the black riders lie there choking and coughing from the smoke. So she ran inside and got some water. As the crowd stared at her with disgust, she continued to go back and forth bringing the victims water. She was the only person who had the courage to be humane. [48]

Although just a child, Janie wouldn't compromise her personal ethics. She wouldn't let those injured people choke.

Leaders' circumstances may not be as drastic as Janie's, but they're faced daily with situations in which they must decide whether to act ethically. They are faced with the temptation to compromise their ethics through political pressure, popularity or friendship. If you're serious about leadership, you must recognize the key to maintaining your standards is to do as Confucius said long ago: "Let the leader show rectitude in his personal character and things will do well, even without directions from him."

---

[48] Adapted from Earl Babbie, *You Can Make a Difference* (New York: St. Martin's Press, 1985), pp 57-58.

EMPOWERMENT WORKSHOP

In what ways have you felt you compromised your ethics? In what kind of circumstances have you given in to the temptation of acting unethically? Do you believe it was justified? Why or why not?

A Look at Unethical Behavior

People get caught up in unethical circumstances for thousands of reasons. We've already looked at a few examples of people who have become victims of poor ethics. But what are the main motivators behind such actions? I believe leaders become victims of corruption through the following means:

Greed

How many times have you seen leaders who were absolutely consumed with greed? Or how many times in the last few years have you read stories about wealthy financiers who initiated leveraged buyouts just so they could cushion their wallets?

Greed comes in three main forms: money, power and fame. You and I could probably come up with hundreds of stories about people who have fallen prey to any one or a combination of those three things. Ben Johnson, the Olympic runner, wanted fame. Richard Nixon wanted power. Manuel Noriega wanted all three. And because of their greed they each acted unethically. Johnson admitted to taking steroids. Nixon was accused of being involved in the Watergate scandal and then lying about it, and Noriega was known to traffic drugs.

129

Poor Judgment

We've probably all been victims of poor judgment which caused us to compromise our ethics. Employers are common victims of lapses in judgment. Let's say, for example, a person comes to interview for an accounting position. The executive senses there's something questionable about the interviewee's character, yet he or she needs an accountant immediately and the person has excellent credentials. The executive hires the person anyway.

Several months later, the employer discovers an unusual amount of money has been channeled out of travel expense accounts. That nagging feeling he or she felt at the interview reemerges. The employer is suddenly caught in the middle of an unethical situation, and after an investigation, realizes the new accountant is the culprit.

Poor judgment is not following your instincts when it comes to principles. Effective leaders know the value of trusting their instincts and never compromising their standards.

Lack of Self-Discipline

I believe lack of self-discipline is the number one cause of most of the sexual scandals and alcohol and drug-related incidents we hear about. People who fail to control their desires and habits reveal a lack of commitment in their lives. Not only do they show little concern for themselves and their bodies, but they also reveal their indifference toward others and the organizations in which they work.

A lack of commitment will carry over into a person's leadership role. Extraordinary leaders need to be dedicated to living disciplined lives. If they fail to keep their personal conduct in check, they will have to face the consequences of negative affects on their leadership abilities.

Types of Unethical Behaviors

Greed, poor judgment and lack of self-discipline are all motivators for unethical behavior. But that's not necessarily what

130

other people observe when they see a leader's unprincipled actions. These motivators can cause several different manifestations of poor ethics. Below are what I consider the most common ways:

Dishonesty

Dishonesty seems to top the list when it comes to poor ethics. Leaders must be honest, not just because it's valuable to their credibility, but because lying never works in the long run. The old saying is true: What goes around comes around. Even Moses knew the consequences of wrongdoing; he told the Gadites and Reubenites that they could be sure their sins would find them out. [49]

Leaders should heed the same advice. Your lies will find you out—someway, somehow and probably when you least expect it. Does that mean leaders should always tell the *absolute* truth? Where do you draw the line between lying and white lying?

If you're serious about being an ethical leader you must determine where that line is. I don't believe leaders should be brutally honest at all times because in some circumstances *tact* must play a role.

For instance, leaders don't lie about how many miles they actually travelled on their last business trip or whether or not they think a colleague's proposal is really a good one. But they do exercise *tact* about the way they tell a colleague the truth about poor eating habits.

White lying to me is a negative term. That's why I prefer to look at it as tact. Extraordinary leaders should not be destructive with the truth, but they should not compromise their standards either.

Acts of Omission

Acts of omission are often overlooked when considering ethics, but I firmly believe this is one of the most serious problems we face. People who neglect to say or do something

---

[49] *The Bible,* New International Version, Numbers 32:23.

about another person's unethical actions commit an act of omission.

Extreme examples of this are instances when people witness muggings or rapes and do nothing about it. Who could forget the story of Kitty Genovese, the New York woman who was stabbed to death as her neighbors watched? Or the hundreds of people, including influential leaders in the United States, who knew early on of the atrocities in the Nazi death camps yet delayed their efforts to stop Hitler?

Acts of omission can be as severe as this, or they can be as "minor" as watching a friend shoplift, ignoring a co-worker altering a time-sheet, or attending an office party where alcohol is served even though it's against regulations.

Silence or simply removing oneself from the situation is not the solution to unethical behavior. Extraordinary leaders make their standards clear, and they have the courage to stand up for what is right.

Illegalities

Once a person is involved with dishonesty or acts of omission, it's easy to become involved in something illegal. Illegalities are not just major crimes like extortion or theft. Leaders who want to make a difference don't become involved in anything that even hints of illegality. They don't cheat on their taxes or recreate receipts. They don't alter documents or scrimp on regulations to save money. They stay on the up-and-up regardless of the benefits not to.

Unscrupulous Tactics

Extraordinary leaders, regardless of what motivates them—money, power or fame—never allow themselves to become entangled in unscrupulous tactics. They don't become sexually involved with or play favorites among their associates. They don't lose their tempers or act in a degrading or immature manner.

It's not necessary for me to go through all the different types of unscrupulous behavior. Most of you understand that being

132

scrupulous means acting honorably, respectably and ethically at all times. You know where you need to draw the line.

Establish Your Personal Ethics

We all have different opinions on what is good or bad, right or wrong. Because we have such differences it's crucial for leaders to determine individually what they believe is ethical. As British philosopher George Edward Moore wrote in his *Principia Ethica* in 1903:

> *"It appears to me that in Ethics, as in all other philosophical studies, the difficulties and disagreements, of which history is full, are mainly due to a very simple cause: namely to the attempt to answer questions without first discovering precisely what question it is you desire to answer."* [50]

One of the first questions you have to ask is, "Where do *I* stand?" Plutarch tells us of the inscription at the Delphic Oracle: "Know thyself." [51] To that wisdom, Shakespeare adds this admonition in a dialogue between Polonius and his son, Laertes:

> *"This above all: to thine own self be true,*
> *And it must follow, as the night the day,*
> *Thou canst not then be false to any man."* [52]

It's vital for you to establish your ethics early and strictly live by them. That way you won't have to fear scandal as a result of your actions. You won't have to fear being "found out," or losing respect because of indifference. Extraordinary leaders are so confident with their ethical standards they *welcome* the opportunity to have them questioned or scrutinized. They know they have nothing to worry about.

---

[50] George Edward Moore, *Principia Ethica* (Cambridge: University Press, 1959), p. vii.

[51] Plutarch, *Moralia*, trans. Frank Cole Babbitt (Cambridge: Harvard University Press, 1928), II, p. 83.

[52] William Shakespeare, "Hamlet," *The Complete Works of William Shakespeare* (Roslyn, N.J.: Walter . Black, 1937), I, iii, p. 1133.

When you're trying to define your standards in any leadership role, first determine what you believe personally. Take into consideration your religious beliefs, your code of conduct and your sense of fairness. No matter how hard you try, you can't separate your personal ethics from your professional ones. If you do, you will lose credibility. After all, it would be hypocritical for leaders to say that they abhor a certain behavior at home then allow it at the office.

If you've never really established a written statement of your ethical standards, I encourage you to do so. It will help you determine exactly where you stand when you're faced with sensitive issues, and it will reveal to you what you believe is important.

To close this chapter, I'd like you to consider the following empowerment workshop. Search yourself. Be direct and thorough. I can assure you this exercise will make a difference in the way you lead.

EMPOWERMENT WORKSHOP

Take the time to write down your ethical standards and what the consequences would be if someone violated those standards.

After you've written those down consider the following unethical situations and determine how you would handle each. How do they rate according to your principles? Did you follow through the way you thought you would?

- One of your co-workers, who's also a good friend, is seeing someone at the office behind his or her spouse's back.

- You discover that someone from another department is using company supplies for personal use.

- One of your clients makes obscene, racial jokes about one of his or her employees.

- A co-worker continually uses foul language, even when carrying on a simple conversation.

8

EMPOWERMENT PRINCIPLE #7
Leaders Strive for Personal Power

"Responsibility gravitates toward him who gets ready for it, and power flows to him and through him who can use it."

—George Walter Fiske [53]

" . . . being powerful is like being a lady. If you have to tell people that you are, you aren't."

—Prime Minister Margaret Thatcher [54]

---

[53] George Sweeting, *Great Quotes & Illustrations* (New York: Word Books, 1985), p. 203.
[54] As quoted by Sheila Murray Bethel, *Making a Difference* (New York: G.P. Putnam's Sons, 1990), p. 167.

The Magnet of Influence

Adolf Hitler and Theodore Roosevelt had totally different outlooks on leadership. Margaret Thatcher and Moammar Gadhafi are like night and day. What makes these people so different? Each of us is unique; we have our own individual qualities and characteristics. But what marks a clear distinction among these leaders is their leadership styles.

Most of us would agree there's a vast difference in tyrannical power and personal power. Hitler and Gadhafi ruled with tyrannical power. Roosevelt and Thatcher maintained great personal power; they were extraordinary leaders. They realized they could not be effective if they abused their power; instead, they used it to gain respect and influence.

Empowerment Principle #7:
Extraordinary leaders strive to attain personal power to influence and empower their workers.

What Is Personal Power?

Even though most of us agree that tyrannical power and personal power are at opposite ends of the spectrum, many of us cannot adequately define personal power. And this is essential for potential leaders if they hope to master the art of influencing and motivating people.

The key to understanding personal power is realizing it has little to do with *how you act toward others*. It has everything to do with *what you do for yourself.* Personal power is based on who you are, not what your position makes you out to be.

I like to consider personal power as the influence leaders have over others. Now I'm not referring to the authoritative influence leaders often hold over the heads of their followers. I'm talking about the influence that creates a bond or link between leader and follower.

Leaders master the process of guiding people's perceptions of them. In the last chapter we discussed how you direct other's perceptions of your credibility with your ethics. Likewise, you guide people's perceptions of your power through interaction. Personal power is not something you learn to achieve in a book; it comes from daily interaction with those your leadership position affects.

Leaders who truly understand the concept of personal power can't receive satisfaction from titles following their names on their doors. *They get satisfaction from using their power to empower others.*

The more leaders understand how to use power, the more effective they will be. An iron fist doesn't move people to action; personal power does. I can assure you the effectiveness of a family, team, club or organization is developed by the example of its leaders.

Personal power is the leader's energy; energy he or she can use to foster power in others. For example, leaders who curtail other people's power for the sake of their egos diminish their individual influence.

Remember, personal power goes hand-in-hand with perception, and perceptions are easily swayed. Perceived power is unconscious power. In other words, people shouldn't be able to notice the power you have. It should be so much a part of your personality that they don't immediately focus on it.

Others should only be able to recognize that you have an incredible amount of *influence*. To be sure your power is something that's unconscious to others, you need to focus on what you do for yourself. You must recognize that:

1. You can only manage yourself.

Leaders cannot manage other people. Consider the relationship between parents and children. At some point in life, parents realize they can't force their children to do what they say. They can only be the kind of example that encourages a specific behavior. The same is true of leaders. When you've mastered self-management, others will naturally follow suit.

2. You can only motivate yourself.

Think about where your personal motivation comes from. Even though at times it may look like you're being motivated by another person, you really are not. *We're the only ones who can unlock the door to our personal motivation.*

It's impossible for a leader to actually motivate another person. The best leaders can do is create such an atmosphere of excitement others buy into that excitement as well. When a leader is enthusiastic about a project or a vision, that enthusiasm is contagious.

3. You can only change yourself.

Change seems to be one of the most unnatural things in the world to human beings, and it can cause more grief and confusion than anything else I know. I won't deny it's difficult for me to change; I agonize over issues requiring me to alter my habits or methods for doing things.

Most people feel the same way. So if it's hard for us to individually go through change, you can bet it's impossible to change others. Remember, your example is what's going to give you unconscious power. When people witness the changes in you, they will be more apt to change themselves.

For example, Mitchell, a customer service manager for a major department store, was known among his subordinates for his loud, ornery disposition. His cantankerousness fostered such a poor work environment the customer service staff reflected this same attitude toward the customers.

When the customers started complaining to upper management, the vice president approached Mitchell about his department's attitude and behavior. He wanted to see changes.

Mitchell believed the problem lay with those employees dealing directly with the customers. So he met with his staff and demanded change. Over a two-week period he tried everything he could think of to get them to change. Nothing worked. It actually got worse.

Eventually, Mitchell realized his orneriness and the way he interacted with his employees was the root of the problem. The workers were only following their leader's example. He decided to try a different approach. He started acting more considerate, patient and approachable, and an amazing thing happened. The same behavior change started occurring among the staff.

Recognizing Destructive Power

Leaders who abuse their power not only risk losing credibility, respect and influence, they also risk losing their leadership position. Psychoanalyst Erich Fromm said, "A lust for power is not rooted in strength but in weakness." [55] I couldn't agree more.

We all have different weaknesses. I've found leaders tend to struggle with four, in particular: ego, self-interest, arrogance and greed. When these are combined with a lust for power, serious problems can arise. Let's take a closer look at each of these types of destructive power.

Ego Power

Egomaniacs are people who are selfish; they're concerned with their individual interests instead of those of others or the

---

[55] Reprinted from Lloyd Cory, *Quotable Quotes* (Wheaton, IL: Victor Books, 1985), p. 292.

organization. When leaders become entrapped by ego power, they fail to focus on visions that place the interests of the organization first. Boosting ego becomes a way of gaining fame.

Regardless of whether the organization becomes successful or another person contributes to its success, the ego-powered leader wants all the glory. These leaders have an unhealthy desire for applause and adoration. They're usually excessively proud of themselves and everything they accomplish.

Henry Ford had ego power. He was known for his iron fist at the Ford Motor Company, and that iron fist was the foundation for his self-glory. He assured no one would gain more prestige or recognition than he did. His reputation was all that mattered.

The truth was Ford received many of his ideas from his employees, yet he rarely gave credit where it was due.

Self-interest Power

Leaders who focus on self-interest power only want to receive personal gain from their leadership roles. They either want more money, recognition or status. Their needs are foremost. Anything that doesn't contribute to their own gratification or increase their own net worth isn't relevant.

Frank Lorenzo, the bold entrepreneur who capitalized on airline deregulation, is a prime example of a leader with self-interest power. Known as the "Pac-Man" of the air industry, he swallowed up six airlines and is considered to have cut every corner, including wages, just so he could make money.

Arrogance Power

When Francois "Papa Doc" Duvalier took over Haiti, he named himself "Prince and Ruler Forever." He was positive nothing was better for the country than what he could provide. He removed the military mentors and established a government that yielded to him alone.

He was so full of arrogance, he refused to allow anyone to challenge his rule. He set up a personal terror squad responsible for seizing, torturing and killing his opponents. He turned the

Haitians into slaves, allowing them to starve, while flaunting his opulent lifestyle in front of them.

Like Papa Doc, leaders who are trapped by arrogance power overvalue themselves. They see themselves as superior to everyone else. This is most commonly reflected in their condescending attitude toward others and their ideas. They're also presumptive and assume authority and privileges where they have no right.

Greed Power

Greed-powered leaders are usually vain and lack discipline. We've talked at great length about greed so it's not necessary to go into it again. Leaders who are motivated by greed get their sense of power from overindulging in whatever brings them the most satisfaction. They can overindulge in authority, money or passion just to name a few.

Hotel manager Leona Helmsley was a greed-powered leader. Her sense of power came from managing several hotels and hoarding as much money as she could. She went so far she organized a scheme to avoid $1.2 million in taxes by billing more than $3 million in personal expenses to Helmsley businesses.

According to the judge who sentenced her for tax fraud, she was motivated by "naked greed." She wanted money and believed she stood above the law to get it.

```
┌─────────────────────────────────────┐
│                                     │
│     EMPOWERMENT WORKSHOP            │
│                                     │
└─────────────────────────────────────┘
```

Reflect on positions of leadership you've held. In what cases have you abused your power? Where have you allowed your motivators to become misaligned with your or the organization's visions or goals.

The Credo of Credibility

Former Speaker of the House Jim Wright, was a Texan with "down-home" qualities that led people to believe he valued honesty and integrity. He was a staunch advocate of enforcing ethical standards. To free our governmental system from unscrupulousness, he vehemently pursued investigations on fellow officials.

His actions, however, created a great deal of media coverage, and suddenly his own ethics came under public scrutiny. People wanted to be sure Wright was on the up-and-up in his own life.

Wright's book, *Reflections of a Public Man,* a collection of several of his old speeches, became the first thing in question. Evidence suggested he deliberately bypassed House limits on speaking fees. He apparently unloaded thousands of copies of the book on lobbyists and other loyalists at $5.95 a copy. But the real kicker was he had cut a 55% royalty deal with the publisher. As a result, he pocketed $38,000 more than the House outside-income limits allowed.

Eventually, the House Speaker was asked to step down for evading the honorarium rule on individual income as well as gaining extra income through the maze of other House rules. What Wright didn't realize was a leader's credibility is wrapped up in his or her use of power. In other words, the way in which he used his power to ensure a respectable atmosphere needed to be congruent with his credibility.

So how can people learn to effectively use their power and how can they recognize when they're abusing it? I believe this can be done by observing the following principles:

1. Leaders must be consistent.

If you're in a leadership position, don't fool yourself into believing people don't watch you. They watch every move you make and everything you say or don't say. If you're inconsistent about the way you handle things, you can bet those following you will have that same problem overall.

Consistency provides a sense of security. If you're consistent, people don't have to fear you will act one way one day and another the next. President Harry Truman was admired for his consistency. Not everyone liked what a tough leader he was, but Truman said what he thought and did what he said. People respected that. There was no reason to doubt that when he said, "The buck stops here," it did.

2. Leaders must provide stability.

By being consistent, leaders reinforce stability. People need to feel assured in their organizational environments. If they're surrounded by indecision, lack of commitment and contradiction, they will doubt the leader's judgment and ability to lead. When people question the stability of their positions they act with apprehension and fear.

In our era of downsizing, many people have felt this lack of stability at work. Several companies have eliminated more than half their middle managers, leaving behind a handful of inexperienced, anxious workers to handle the reorganization.

When Kodak Canada restructured, their leaders recognized how critical maintaining stability was. They didn't want people fearing their names would be on a lay-off list the next day. They provided an environment free from secrets. They made sure all employees knew what was happening and gave them the opportunity to provide input concerning their jobs.

146

As a result, a stronger, more effective work environment emerged.

3. Leaders must meet others' significant expectations.

It's vital for effective leaders to know and understand what people expect from them. We all require differing amounts of supervision, encouragement and discipline. It's your job as a leader to determine what those amounts are and to assure they're adequately provided. People will feel more secure knowing their leaders are concerned about their individual needs and consistently try to meet them.

John B. Fery, CEO of Boise Cascade, a corrugated container plant, does this. He visits the plant on a regular basis, meets with the workers and asks about their concerns. It's not uncommon to find him talking with the workers on the line. He welcomes questions on all topics because he wants to meet the needs of his company as well as his employees' expectations. As a result, his workers feel stable and know that he cares about them.

4. Leaders must be trustworthy.

Trust is probably the most fragile aspect of developing relationships. And leadership is all about developing the kind of relationships that foster an empowered environment. Without the trust of their followers, leaders haven't an ounce of credibility. Most of us know how hard it is to gain people's trust. Hopefully, only a few of us know how easily it's lost.

Extraordinary leaders do everything they can to prevent losing trust. They work hard to keep their promises, support their followers, remain sensitive and maintain confidentiality.

EMPOWERMENT WORKSHOP

> **List those areas of your life where you can become more consistent, provide more stability, meet others' expectations and be more trustworthy. Specifically project how it will affect the outcome of your leadership.**

Mastering the Balancing Act

Learning to balance wisdom and power is the key to overcoming power abuse. Personal power is all about empowering others to be activators in the leadership process. Leaders enhance their power by focusing on these strategies:

Mobilizing Others

Mobilization is when people function beyond simply doing a task to effectively and strategically use their own power. In other words, mobilization transforms people into power sources and makes them partners in the organizational vision. The way we prepare men to become soldiers in the military is a good example of mobilization.

Many men enlist as boys, knowing nothing about disciplining themselves let alone performing any type of leadership role. But through mobilization they become leaders of themselves, of a unit and of a country.

As an officer I worked to enhance other men's leadership skills so, if it were necessary, those men could depend on their own knowledge and decision making abilities to achieve the organizational vision. I watched men transform themselves for action.

148

Extraordinary leaders know the value of maximizing the potential of the people they lead. They can mobilize them into power-packed coalitions. When special forces teams are formed in the military, these coalitions are evident.

The leaders of these teams work with a select group of soldiers. They learn the potential of each person and target his strengths into a specific area. As a result, they are prepared to handle the most challenging, often dangerous missions with little direction.

Removing Leadership Walls

Leadership walls can form for a number of reasons. Most often they're recognized as the barricades of authority that separate leaders from people. Effective leaders learn not to allow the walls of superiority to enter their relationships. They refuse to allow the "poshness" of their position (if it has some) to get in the way.

In other words, they don't let their secretaries call their friends to set up lunch for them just so they can show off their status. They don't let their aides dial the phone for them in airports. Leaders who know the value of breaking down walls walk around *with* their people.

They make sure a sense of equality is always present. They lead like George Washington did during the Revolutionary War. He didn't go somewhere to live in comfort while his men suffered through the harsh winter. He stayed with them and was as cold and hungry as they were.

Extraordinary leaders don't need lavish coddling to reassure them in their roles and provide them with a sense of importance. They know their importance comes from the way others perceive them and the way they work as a team to reach their goals.

Practicing Leadership by Walking Around

This strategy is for those people who think leadership is sitting in a penthouse office high above where the work goes on. You will learn what's really going on in your organization only

149

if you take the time to walk with your associates and communicate openly with them.

One of the best examples of a leader who "walked around" was Sam Bird.[56] Sam was a 26-year-old captain in Vietnam, and he never let himself become a victim of positional power. He was a leader who was true to the term personal power.

Sam was the type of leader who dug trenches, filled sandbags, strung wire and set up shelters right alongside his men. He knew them each by name and knew about their families. He cultivated a sense of family in the shambles of a war because he knew the value of leadership by walking around.

Joseph E. Antonini, the CEO of K Mart stores, is another man who believes in leadership by walking around. He visits all the K Mart stores so he can always have a feel for his business. He walks the floors suggesting ways to rejuvenate sales. He provides managers and sales clerks with marketing suggestions and display alterations. He checks the stock rooms. Most importantly, he spends time talking with the customers and workers.

Communicating

Communication is the process of getting to where other people are. It's sharing knowledge, information, feelings and ideas. Leaders who openly communicate with those in their organizations discover they've tapped into an invaluable source of energy.

When leaders help people realize their opinions are important, they open the door to enormous opportunity. People who feel they can approach their leaders with ideas, suggestions and criticisms without fear of reprisal are better workers. They become empowered faster, and are willing to venture into the new frontiers you lay before them.

Communication is the only way leaders can monitor their followers' progress and meet everyone's expectations. We will

---

[56] B.T. Collins, "The Courage of Sam Bird," *Reader's Digest*, May 1989, p. 49-54.

focus specifically on the assets of good communication skills in Chapter 9.

Personal power is something that's attainable by ordinary people. It's a strategic way of conforming yourself and your habits into new techniques that focus on others. It starts with being a living example and fostering an attitude that manifests selfless power. It's the best way to see immediate progress toward your vision, and it's the only way to insure that you will become and remain an extraordinary leader.

EMPOWERMENT WORKSHOP

Determine where in your leadership position you're trying to improve your personal power. How can you put these strategies to use? Where do you have leadership walls? Don't limit yourself to just walls of authority. Really search yourself to see what other kinds of walls you may be unconsciously creating.

If you have a hard time being honest with yourself or thinking of areas where you can improve, enlist the help of a friend you trust and ask him or her to evaluate you. Have the person list those areas where he or she feels you fall short in mobilizing, breaking down walls and communicating.

9

EMPOWERMENT PRINCIPLE #8
Leaders Make a Difference Through the Power of Communication

"Communication is depositing a part of yourself in another person."

—Anonymous [57]

"Communication creates meaning for people. Or should. It's the only way any group, small or large, can become aligned behind the overarching goals of an organization."

—Warren Bennis and Burt Nanus [58]

---

[57] George Sweeting, *Great Quotes & Illustrations* (Waco, Texas: Word Books, 1985), p. 66.
[58] Warren Bennis and Burt Nanus, *Leaders: The Strategies For Taking Charge* (New York: Harper & Row, 1985), p. 43.

The Veins and Arteries of an Organization

Open communication lines between leaders and followers are the veins and arteries transporting the vital energy necessary to sustain an organization at maximum potential. Used effectively, communication can be one of the leader's most powerful tools.

Communication skills not only forge productive relationships, they also promote understanding which results in a desired action. Good leaders want their associates to embrace their inspired visions. To accomplish that goal, leaders must first communicate their visions. Good leaders also want their organizational environments to be full of healthy relationships. Again, communication has to be the first step.

Empowerment Principle #8:
Extraordinary leaders use communication skills to enhance their leadership abilities and create powerful environments that thrive on attaining the organizational vision.

Leaders know the value of effective discourse for themselves, but more importantly they know the impact it has on those they're leading. Below are four major ways in which your communication skills will make a difference:

1. *They motivate people.*

Leaders who communicate effectively set up motivational opportunities. People who know how to share enthusiasm have a better chance of helping others become enthusiastic about their causes.

Remember, it's impossible to actually motivate another person. The door to motivation has to be opened from the *inside*. You're the only one who can open your door. Once your motivation door is open, you will be able to encourage others to open theirs.

When I conduct an orchestra, I'm responsible for communicating to the musicians a sense of excitement about the piece they're playing. Otherwise the music will sound dull and lifeless, or worse, mechanical. The main goal of an orchestra is to create music that reveals the feelings of the composer in such a way that the audience gets involved in it. But before musicians can inspire others to feel the music, they must feel it themselves.

Through my communication with the musicians, I can spread my understanding and enthusiasm for the way a piece should be expressed. Only then will orchestra members be able to combine their efforts into a performance that fosters the same feelings in the audience. Nothing I say will actually motivate the violinists or the trombonists to play with more depth and feeling. But the way I communicate through my conducting can certainly encourage it.

2. *They establish an environment of mutual trust and cooperation.*

Good communication skills are the glue holding an organization together. Have you ever been in an organization where a rumor is being spread about changes or cutbacks? If the environment isn't conducive to open communication or employees can't get information from internal sources, that rumor can create a great deal of animosity or fear among workers. People who open the lines of communication will see results in mutual trust and cooperation.

156

As a leader you will have more success getting people to do things if they trust you. People who feel comfortable about airing their opinions and complaints voluntarily contribute more to the organization.

3. They focus the mission.

Clear communication also helps leaders zero in on the organizational mission. When people know what the leader's goals are and what is expected of them, they will put more effort into making that mission a reality.

Open, honest communication allows room for constructive criticism, which is the only way leaders can fine-tune their visions, goals and objectives into workable, attainable missions. Leaders who understand the role of good communication also know its advantages.

- They will receive more ideas and more support.

- They will be more attuned to potential problems.

- They will encourage more participation.

- They will be able to improve their own leadership skills and the function of the organization.

- They will cultivate strong bonds of unity among their workers.

4. They allow for mediation and resolution.

Leaders who communicate well, and encourage the same from others, have refined one of the main principles in the art of problem-solving. No group or organization is free from problems, and leaders who wish to improve their sense of awareness need to know the value of creating a comfortable environment that welcomes true communication.

Leaders can use their communication skills to mediate in sensitive situations, discuss controversial issues and resolve problems that have formed.

The Art of Communication

Effective leaders from all walks of life have used the art of communication to change minds, laws and nations; they've encouraged growth and success. They've made a difference by helping small children understand the concept of right and wrong or advocating a movement to address the nationwide problem of the homeless.

When Martin Luther King, Jr. organized a boycott of segregated buses in Selma, Alabama, he motivated people to become involved in one of the most significant issues of history. Through his skillful communication he spearheaded the civil rights movement.

When King said he had a dream, he was focused on a mission, and he knew how to communicate through word pictures to capture the nation's attention. He convinced people to become involved with his cause by transmitting his personal desire and commitment to racial freedom:

> *"I have a dream that one day on the red hills of Georgia the sons of former slaves and the sons of former slave owners will be able to sit down together at the table of brotherhood."* [59]

Abraham Lincoln wasn't a fancy person or a master of elocution, and he certainly didn't have the charisma of Martin Luther King, Jr. But he was sincere, and he was motivated to his cause. He knew what the people wanted and he genuinely wanted to see those desires become reality.

His Gettysburg Address was a mere 266 words long and followed a long talk by one of the nation's most highly respected orators, Edward Everett. Lincoln's message left a lasting mark on people of all generations, yet Everett's is hardly remembered. That says a lot about the effects of quality communication.

---

[59] As quoted by Sheila Murray Bethel, *Making A Difference* (New York: G. P. Putnam's Sons, 1990) p. 195.

Communication and Failure

No one likes to fail. Yet few people really try to improve the one thing that can prevent them from failing as leaders—their communication skills. According to the *Wall Street Journal,* poor communication is a significant reason people fail at managing or leading: "Poor interpersonal skills represent the single biggest reason for failure—especially in the early and middle stages of a [leader's] career—and the most crucial flaw to recognize and remedy." [60]

In these days of intense competition, it's crucial for leaders to communicate effectively for maximum impact. The reality is: Communication can mean the difference in making or losing money and in gaining or losing credibility. Why? We constantly misunderstand messages.

We experience degrees of misunderstanding every day. We leave meetings not knowing exactly what we're supposed to do. We listen to presidential addresses only to come away with ears full of rhetoric, and we strain our relationships because we don't know how to communicate what we really mean to other people. Muddled communication and sloppy dialogue are almost epidemic.

I'm not going to disillusion you. Getting through to people is probably one of the hardest things in the world. Have you ever felt the frustration of explaining something to someone who just couldn't grasp what you were saying? I have many times, especially as a teacher.

Communication breakdowns can occur for any number of reasons. The key to avoiding them lies in understanding how they occur and learning to combat the problems as they arise. I've discovered communication breakdowns develop because of:

Poor Signal Reception

Most of us know what it's like to watch a television program when the station has poor signal reception. There's often a

---

[60] Carol Hymowitz, "Five Main Reasons Why Managers Fail," *The Wall Street Journal,* May 2, 1988, Section 2, p. 1.

snowy appearance to the picture and an annoying crackling sound. We experience sensory problems when this happens, and it usually alters how much or how well we hear the program.

Poor signal reception can be an obstacle to effective communication. It affects what we hear when another person is speaking. Where does that interference come from? All of us have the ability to shut our minds on and off when we feel the need. In other words, we permit interference if we don't want to hear what another person is saying. When we do this, we allow our minds to process information through what I call our listening filters. A little later in the chapter we will look more closely at what these listening filters are.

Disinterest is another common reason we experience poor signal reception. If we don't particularly care about a topic or it seems too technical to handle, we allow our "television screens" to fuzz it out or we turn on our listening filters.

Improper Translation

For the communication process to be completed effectively, we must attach meaning to the words, sounds and ideas we hear from other people. Attaching meaning is what promotes understanding. It's through this process we're able to verify receiving the correct information. The problem with message reception is that people often attach the wrong meaning to messages.

We all experience situations when we try to get a point across and through feedback realize the other person has gotten the wrong idea. Immediately we say, "That's not what I meant." Because of the complexity of the English language, it's easy to have our messages incorrectly translated.

For example, the word "deck" can mean a wooden porch, a pack of cards, a part of a ship or a layer of clouds. It can even mean forcefully knocking someone down, decorating or dressing elegantly. With that many meanings attached to one word, there's no doubt it can be hard to get messages across.

Even the *way* we say something can cause a person to misinterpret what we're saying. Consider the differences in this sentence depending upon the speaker's voice inflections.

"Bill threw the ball that broke the window." (This could be just a statement of fact.)

*"**Bill** threw the ball that broke the window."* (This could be a statement of accusation.)

*"Bill threw the ball that **broke** the window?"* (This could be a statement of disbelief.)

If we don't practice good communication and listening skills we will jump to the wrong conclusions. When this happens messages are improperly received.

Inaccurate Assessment

After we translate a message, we go through a process of evaluating it. In other words, we assess the message by either accepting it or rejecting it. When we accept information, we use it immediately or store it away for further use. When we reject it, we filter it out altogether. Many of us tend to listen selectively and, as a result, we evaluate messages inaccurately because we only have a small portion of the information necessary for true understanding.

For example, Mark, a member of a local civic organization, was in charge of organizing the annual fund raising carnival. Andrew, the president of the club, wanted to try out some new ideas so he asked to meet with the carnival chairman. When Andrew started suggesting some ideas, Mark turned on his listening filter.

Mark concluded the president didn't like his ideas, so he was telling Mark how to do the job. Had Andrew been concentrating on the message, the chairman would have correctly evaluated what was being said. Mark wouldn't have felt incompetent. Instead, Mark would have realized Andrew was pleased with his contributions and was

161

making the suggestions because he valued Mark's feedback.

One-sidedness is another common way we fail to assess messages accurately. We all have opinions and beliefs on certain matters, and assessing information from our personal perspectives can lead to serious misunderstandings.

Emotional Reaction

If you're like most people, you've been in situations where another person said something and it made you angry. What, exactly, made you angry? Human beings are made up of emotions, and those emotions cause us to react verbally and non-verbally to the way others communicate to us.

We can be provoked by tone of voice, word choice and body language. Breakdowns start to occur when we shut a person out because of what he or she is saying. You know when you're doing it. You may start to think of a rebuttal right away. You may fold your arms across your chest, or even leave the room.

Leaders who learn to remove themselves emotionally when they're communicating, or at least learn to keep their emotions in check assure they hear the entire message. Otherwise, their emotions can shadow the true meaning of a conversation.

Becoming a Successful Communicator

Learning to be a successful communicator begins with analyzing your intentions. Abraham Lincoln didn't just get up and ad lib a few comments at the cemetery in Gettysburg. He spent time and energy thinking about what message he wanted to send, and he left the nation with the impression and motivation he wanted.

People who wish to become extraordinary leaders must decide what impact or impression they want to make *before* they attempt to communicate and then work toward that objective in a strategic manner. To be sure you understand what you want to accomplish, consider the four most common goals of communication:

Understanding

People communicate because they want another person to comprehend certain information. They want people to capture a personal understanding of it. Teachers and ministers aim for this goal most of the time.

Agreement

Obtaining agreement is a method of communicating in which one person wishes to convince another of his or her beliefs, ideas or viewpoints. Debaters and lobbyists most often use this method of communication.

Action

When people communicate to achieve action, they want results from what they say. They want to persuade a person to do something. Leaders often use this type of communication to organize projects and reach goals. Fundraisers and salespeople often communicate to ensure action.

Information

When someone lacks the knowledge to handle a situation or perform a task, he or she asks questions to seek information.

EMPOWERMENT WORKSHOP

When you're getting ready to communicate, evaluate your intentions. Do you know exactly what you wish to achieve? If not, how can you ensure it?

Once leaders are sure of their communicative intentions, they must create the proper environment for success. Extraordinary leaders follow these rules:

1. Leaders are impartial observers.

This goes along with what I said earlier about separating yourself from the emotions communication can instigate. Effective leaders learn the art of an unbiased approach to communication so they can get to the real meaning behind messages. Often people take preconceived notions and prejudices into a communication situation and allow them to alter the entire event.

We can miss a lot of information by being subjective. A clear focus on the person speaking and the situation at hand can ensure better understanding.

2. Leaders never assume anything.

Effective leaders never assume their audiences know anything about what they're communicating. For instance, if you're talking to a group of musicians about a Stradivarius they would understand what you meant. To any other audience you would probably refer to the instrument as a violin.

That's not to say you should simplify your information every time you speak to someone. Some situations may not require you to be as thorough as others, so leaders need to improve their discernment abilities to know when it's necessary to provide more detailed explanations.

The critical rule is: always remember others may not have the grasp you do on the information you're presenting. Therefore, you shouldn't leave out information you might think is minor. That "minor" information could very well provide a great deal of insight to the listener.

3. Leaders are never victims of small-talk.

Small-talk can be a deadly trap for leaders. Leaders must determine when courteous small-talk is acceptable and when they're using it as a crutch. Often, leaders will want to ask a person to do a task; they will fill the conversation with small-talk to break the ice but never actually explain the reason for the request.

164

Small-talk can easily hide the purpose of a discussion if the communicator is not careful. If used at all, small-talk should be an afterthought in a conversation. It then becomes a way for the leader to show personal concern for others.

4. Leaders are direct.

When people are uncomfortable with a subject or they're hesitant to request something of another, they sometimes skirt issues. In other words, they're too evasive to actually communicate their messages. Most people who are consistently indirect don't want to offend or anger others. But leaders know that directness is the best way to achieve sound results.

The Single, Most Common Communication Breakdown

Listening is the one aspect of the communication process people do, or should do, more often than any other. Therefore, it's only logical that listening problems head the column of major communication breakdowns. Statistics reveal that we generally spend 45% of our total communicating time listening and only 30% of it speaking. Greek philosopher Diogenes Laertius once said, "We have two ears and only one tongue in order that we may hear more and speak less." [61] There's great wisdom in that statement.

People need to realize that much of their leading will be done through listening. The key to effective communication then is to become attuned to *listening* and not just *hearing*. People have a natural tendency to hear what they want to hear. They use their listening filters. Leaders need to become acutely aware of this inherent weakness and train themselves to overcome it. Let's look at what listening filters are and why we use them.

---

[61] Eleanor Doan, *The New Speaker's Sourcebook* (Grand Rapids, Michigan: Zondervan Books, 1968), . 239.

Listening filters are our minds' unique mechanism for tuning in and tuning out. I mentioned this mental phenomenon earlier. Because our speaking and listening rates are drastically different, we use this mechanism a great deal. We can only talk so fast, yet our minds race ahead of our words to provide us more ideas. Because of our mind's ability to race ahead, we can listen much faster than we can speak. Basically, it's impossible for the speaker to keep up with the other person's listening rate. So it's not uncommon for people to become bored with a conversation.

Why We Use Filters

Let's look at the five main reasons people use their listening filters. Most of them are unconscious habits that can be controlled with practice and discipline.

Poor Concentration

Researchers say that the average concentration span in a normal adult is 20 minutes. Many of us can't concentrate that long because we simply haven't taken the time to properly discipline ourselves. Our fast-paced society allows us to get bored too easily. We expect things to happen quickly, and if a conversation takes too long we become disinterested. It's especially difficult for us to concentrate if we believe the information we're hearing is irrelevant, too technical or too difficult to understand.

Diversions

Diversions come in all shapes and forms—the telephone, the secretary, the up-coming meeting you haven't prepared for or even the dinner party you're planning. When we allow diversions to distract us from the conversation at hand, we process information through our listening filters.

Daydreaming

We've all experienced daydreaming. It happens when conversations become too long, too involved or too boring. I can remember (not proudly) daydreaming in meetings when I was

166

in the military because I was disinterested in the subject being discussed. If it was a topic that didn't appear to involve me too much, I let myself go a million miles away to something I felt was more pleasant.

Preconceptions

We come into every conversation with a set of beliefs, values and opinions. Those are often the factors that control our listening filters. For example, if you're on the Pro-life side of the abortion issue, and a Pro-choice advocate comes to your town to speak, you will quite likely go to the speech with a lot of preconceptions. You may not hear much the person has to say because your filter has already determined what you will choose to hear on the issue.

Hasty Judgment

Have you ever been listening to a conversation and suddenly you *knew* what the other person was going to say, and that you didn't like it, so you activated your filter? That's called jumping to conclusions. Some people make hasty judgments before the other person even has a chance to speak.

These judgments can be based on the way a person looks or is dressed. They may also be determined by the person's body language. For instance, a listener might assume the speaker's arms folded across his or her chest means the information is not something he or she wants to hear.

The Benefits of Receptive Listening

Effective leaders know the value of spending more of their time listening than talking. Hearing your own voice all the time will get you nowhere in the long run. Innovation and growth come from brainstorming and holding conversations with other people. Receptive listening provides leaders with excellent means for cultivating the ordinary into the extraordinary including the following:

Knowledge

Leaders who listen learn something new every day about their people, their problems and their organizations. They know that through all the white noise they're surrounded with there's an ounce of wisdom in everything that's said. Something may not be well said, but wise leaders know how to sift through the racket and listen for those tidbits that can enrich their lives.

Awareness

Leaders who concentrate on keeping their ears open and their mouths shut gain one of the most important leadership qualities—awareness. Awareness is having insight into others' feelings, motives, desires and actions. When leaders allow their listening skills to provide them with awareness, they have an easier time leaving their personal perceptions or judgments behind. It helps them look more objectively at situations that may otherwise be difficult to handle.

Opportunity

Listening is the best way for leaders to get to know those who work for them. It also allows them to attune to new ideas and suggested changes offered by other people. Those suggestions could mean increased profits, improved production or better relationships. Extraordinary leaders take advantage of every opportunity they hear about, and listening is the only way to do that.

True Understanding

Leaders who listen actively focus on the message at hand. They refuse to allow misconceptions to hinder their communication. People who make an effort to really hear what others are saying don't allow their filters to activate, and they don't let their defenses rise. True understanding is total clarity; it's not having to say, "I thought you said . . ."

Developing a Listening Strategy

Extraordinary leaders incorporate a listening strategy to help them get the most out of what they hear. They control their listening filters and master the skill of strategic listening through practice and dedication.

Listening must be thought of as a creative process. An average person can't pick up a saxophone for the first time and play it flawlessly. Likewise, leaders can't expect themselves to be perfect listeners after reading this chapter. It takes total concentration and strict discipline to improve your listening skills. Below I've listed some of the strategies that have been most effective for me.

- **Refuse to be a self-centered listener.** Don't just listen to what you want to hear. Fix your concentration on the speaker at all times.

- **Remain alert.** Force yourself to focus your attention continually on the ideas being communicated. When you're tired or upset, try, if possible, to reschedule meetings dealing with difficult subjects so you can handle such issues when you're mentally alert.

- **Don't trust your memory.** Even though our brains are able to remember practically everything we hear in a lifetime, we don't know how to make use of that ability. Take notes when you're listening to someone. It will help you stay focused on the topic and provide a memory aid.

- **Look at the speaker.** Many times we get distracted because we lose eye contact with the person we're communicating with. Maintaining eye contact will also help you "hear" more than just the words being spoken. You may be able to pick up information from facial expressions and body language.

- **Don't interrupt.** Extraordinary leaders know that when they're listening, their ideas and opinions don't matter. So

169

wait until the other person stops talking before you offer your opinion. It's a good practice to be sure you can summarize what the speaker has said before you begin talking. Also, don't try to finish sentences for slow speakers. Control your urge to hurry them or monopolize the conversation.

- **Always verify facts.** Remembering to do this will keep you from jumping to conclusions. Wait until the person has finished, paraphrase what was said and confirm that you have interpreted the correct meaning.

- **Put yourself in the speaker's shoes.** If you train yourself to try and see the issue from the speaker's point of view, you will avoid filtering out information that goes against your opinions.

- **Remove distractions.** Don't allow yourself to be distracted when you need to actively listen. Hold your phone calls, close the door, move closer to the speaker, look away from other activity and move papers you were working on out of the way.

- **Hold the rein on your emotions.** Know what words and issues make you angry, and recognize that it's the subject not the *speaker* that's getting to you. Focus on the content, and if you become annoyed, ask the speaker to explain the information a different way or use different words to make it clearer.

If you consistently use these techniques, over time you will notice a marked difference in your perceptions. You will realize you were missing out on a lot of important information that could have made an impact on your organization or leadership role.

Take some time before you move on to the next chapter to complete the following empowerment workshop. The benefits of active listening are something that no leader should be without.

EMPOWERMENT WORKSHOP

Rate yourself as a communicator. Use a scale 1 (low rating) to 5 (high rating).

1. I always know my communication intentions before I speak.

2. I strive to achieve an environment of open communication.

3. I can easily recognize when I'm having a communication breakdown.

4. I always maintain control of my emotions when I'm communicating.

5. I'm always observing the ins and outs of my organization or the people with whom I'm working.

6. I limit my small-talk and avoid being evasive.

7. I never interrupt another person who's speaking.

8. I always focus on the speaker so I can more clearly understand the message I'm receiving.

9. I assume every person has something worthwhile to say.

10. I concentrate on *hearing* what the other person is saying and use strategies to maintain my focus.

10

EMPOWERMENT PRINCIPLE #9
Leaders Thrive on Innovation

"The spirit of venture is lost in the inertia of a mind against change."

—*Alfred P. Sloan* [62]

"If [potential leaders and innovators] have the will to live up to their potential, and the rest of us have the gumption to follow them, we might finally find our way out of this bog we're in."

—*Warren Bennis* [63]

---

[62] Alfred P. Sloan, *My Years With General Motors* (Garden City, NY: Doubleday, 1964), p. xxii.
[63] Warren Bennis, *Why Leaders Can't Lead* (San Francisco: Jossey-Bass Publishers, 1989), p. 30.

The Source of Survival

Experts say innovation will be a leader's main source of survival in the '90s and beyond. Leaders will no longer be able to depend on doing things the way they've always done them. Change is too fast. Competition is too great. We cannot escape it. Focusing on innovation is our only way out.

Because of competitive demand, leaders are forced to initiate changes in their environments. It's no longer easy to "keep up with the Joneses." Businesses compete with the Japanese market. Non-profit organizations strive to raise more money than any one else. Schools fight to have the best sports teams. Even our neighbors compete with each other to have the best looking yard.

We've gone from healthy competition to maniacal concentration on winning. We can't just sell harder, work longer or slightly alter our leadership approaches. It takes much more than that to survive.

The key to innovation is creating an environment of C-H-A-N-G-E, an environment with all the necessary ingredients for continued success, including the following:

Challenge

If leaders want to foster creative environments, they must have a sense of challenge. They must have a strong desire to conquer even the most tricky circumstances. Being innovative *is* challenging. Few people can suggest great ideas time after time with little or no effort. But when leaders focus on the thrill of meeting a challenge they can make innovation exciting and worth striving for.

High Incentive

Before you can motivate yourself or others to be more innovative, you have to provide some form of incentive. In other words, what makes coming up with new ideas worthwhile? Will it increase the organization's profits? Maybe it will make money for you personally, like Stew Leonard's One Idea Club does for his employees. Any new idea they contribute can make $10 to $100 for them, depending on the results of the idea.

Active Contribution

Innovation will not occur in organizations if leaders are not 100% involved in it. Participation generates results. An environment that draws people in and encourages them to submit their ideas cultivates innovation. When people see leaders actively involved and excited about discovering new and different ways for bettering the organization, they will follow the example.

No Fear

An environment conducive to creating innovative ideas is free from fear. That means people don't fear being ridiculed for suggesting an idea or failing if their idea doesn't work. They have a no-risk guarantee their ideas will be heard and considered.

Growth Potential

Leaders aiming to create innovative environments see the value in establishing growth potential. For example, people need to see how their activities will contribute to their personal growth and the growth of the organization. How are they assured their ideas will be considered? Will their ideas bring them the deserved recognition?

176

Expectation

When leaders expect innovative ideas they foster an environment that welcomes fresh input. Traditional leadership techniques invite leaders to sit on their high horses and crack the whip. They rarely look for ideas from the "little people."

If you're serious about getting creative suggestions, dispel that myth. The best suggestions often come from the front line. That's where people see problems and the best solutions first hand.

Let everyone in the organization know you value their contributions. Show them how serious you are. Start by making your own contributions, then watch as others become encouraged to do the same.

Breaking the Ice

Innovation can be scary. It represents change, and we all know how unpleasant change can be. Innovation must start with encouragement. In other words, leaders need to break the ice and constantly reaffirm how valuable others' contributions are to them and to the organization. I've discovered these three suggestions help foster that affirmation:

1. Encourage input.

Innovation goes hand-in-hand with motivation. Something has to inspire a person to be creative, right? Well, most of the time. People need to be encouraged to contribute ideas and changes. Extraordinary leaders recognize this as a vital part of their jobs. They probe their workers' minds with carefully constructed questions to draw out the insightful ideas they have.

When people realize leaders are genuinely interested in their opinions, they will offer them regularly. A good way to assure this input is to set up a program where individuals are rewarded for constructive suggestions.

177

```
EMPOWERMENT WORKSHOP
```

List five ways in which you could personally encourage others to offer their input whether it's in your role as a parent, civic leader, teacher, student council president or other type of leader.

2. *Properly acknowledge contributions.*

Proper acknowledgement means taking time to show your appreciation. If you want great ideas, you have to let people know they're appreciated and give them the credit they deserve. Follow through by personally thanking and recognizing people for their suggestions.

If your child washes and waxes your car, most likely you will shower him or her with appreciation and recognize the effort with a reward. If a member of the Lion's club offers a suggestion to make your job as president easier, you should do the same.

You may also want to let people know that even if their ideas aren't useable at the present time, they're kept in a working file for later use. Be attuned to other people's feelings, and be sure to do the little things to assure them of their value to the organization.

3. *Be innovative yourself.*

Nothing is more encouraging than seeing leaders put as much effort into a task as they expect from other people. People model after their leaders; if they see you developing new ideas, they will work harder to come up with their own.

Discipline yourself to suggest five new ideas a week. Share them with others, then ask the same from them. When people see you're serious about the program and you're willing to

178

share your suggestions, good or bad, they will be more willing to do the same.

Embarking on a Mission

I realize leaders have one of the hardest jobs in the world; they must work constantly to encourage people to do things because *they* want to do them. Because leaders face such a challenge motivating people, they must embark on a mission of innovation. That mission involves adjusting your style and environment to incorporate these steps:

1. Start a method for locating sources.

New ideas don't conveniently drop out of thin air. We can't always sit down to brainstorm and be assured of coming up with something exceptional. Leaders realize early in their careers they aren't the only sources for innovation. Some of the best ideas come from other people, companies or publications. People who wish to become extraordinary leaders take advantage of as many additional sources of ideas as they can locate.

Stew Leonard knew one of his main sources was his competition. That's why he regularly sent his people to other stores. His employees could then tell him what the competitor was doing right that their company could do as well or better.

179

EMPOWERMENT WORKSHOP

> **What sources other than those people you work with and organizations like yours could provide you additional insight on innovative methods you could incorporate?**

2. *Be the first one to start gathering ideas.*

I can't stress this enough. Leaders need to be the activators in any strategy they pursue. If you're serious about becoming innovative, start walking your talk. Don't expect everyone else to do the work. By working side-by-side, you will build a solid sense of unity.

Start by keeping a personal journal of all the ideas you come up with. Let your yellow pad be the storage battery for all your inspiration. When you put your visions on paper, you capture them and hold them in readiness to energize your actions.

Don't be afraid to write every idea that comes to mind. Your yellow pad is non-judgmental. It won't say "That's a stupid idea." Remember, the only stupid idea is the one never suggested. If you keep your pad charged with creative ideas, you will find it to be a potent power source, providing innovative energy.

3. *Don't be afraid to experiment.*

Experimentation is what extraordinary leadership is all about. If you're a person who's hesitant to try new things then you can give up attempting to be innovative. Innovation involves a willingness to experience unique changes regardless of their outcome. Remember, "If you do what you've always done, you will get what you've always gotten."

180

4. Develop teams.

According to authors and leadership specialists James M. Kouzes and Barry Z. Posner, teamwork is essential to the productivity of an organization. "It is the key that leaders use to unlock the energies and talents available in their organization." [64] When people's energies and talents are unlocked, great things can happen because creativity thrives.

Undoubtedly, things can go stale in groups and organizations. Your own ideas may sound dry and lifeless. Team-building is the solution to that. When people work in a combined effort, it's much easier to develop fresh input.

5. Encourage risk-taking.

A willingness to take risks means not fearing the unknown. Extraordinary leaders are pioneers in unknown frontiers. Helen Keller once said, "Life is either a daring adventure or it is nothing." [65] I couldn't agree more. Can you imagine what an adventure her life was?

Miracles can happen if people are willing to take risks. Anne Sullivan was willing to take a risk on a blind, deaf and mute child, and what a miracle that child's life turned out to be. In a time when blindness and deafness were often considered a family disgrace, Helen could have become a recluse. Instead, she had the courage to become an extraordinary leader.

In the 1970s, a medical researcher named Gabriel Nahas also knew the value of risk-taking. Even though his life was threatened repeatedly and people all over the country called him a fascist, Nahas remained firm in his convictions.

He knew the affects of drug use, particularly marijuana, were harmful to the body, and he was

---

[64] James M. Kouzes and Barry Z. Posner, *The Leadership Challenge* (San Francisco: Jossey-Bass Publishers, 1987), p. 135.

[65] As quoted by Sheila Murray Bethel, *Making A Difference* (New York: G.P. Putnam's Sons, 1990), p. 145.

willing to do anything to prevent marijuana from becoming a "decriminalized" drug. Years later people discovered he was right. Because of his persistence he became an extraordinary leader, the hero for the national parent movement for drug-free children. [66]

6. Learn from mistakes.

One day while Thomas Edison was working on creating an incandescent light, he was confronted by an assistant who lamented about having completed some five hundred experiments to find an acceptable filament without any results. The inventor gave his assistant a warm smile and assured him they had achieved some results; they had discovered five hundred potential solutions that would not work. Edison clearly wasn't afraid of failing.

Many people view their mistakes as failures instead of what they really are—learning experiences. Consider this story about a line worker at a products company.

Paul was responsible for pouring the mold for a certain number of containers per day. One day, as he was reviewing his records, he discovered several of his containers were failing final inspection tests. He checked his own work to find the production error, but he could find nothing.

When he studied the containers more closely he noticed some of them had small bubbles along the bottom rim. He reheated one container, reshaped the rim and ran it back through the test. It passed.

Since the high percentage of failed containers was reflecting badly on his production, Paul decided to do a little research. He wanted to know where the bubbles were coming from. On his breaks he observed some of the other production divisions. In the metal division he noticed they were pulling the hot metal casts out of the furnace too early.

---

[66] Peggy Mann, "Dogged Crusader Against Drugs," *Reader's Digest,* May 1989, pp. 102-106.

182

When Paul approached the supervisors with his observation, they were angered by his "meddling." Company policy required them to heat the casts five minutes, so that's what they were going to do.

Paul was only interested in decreasing the number of defective containers. He wanted to turn a mistake into an improvement. But no one else wanted anything to do with it. None of the supervisors wanted to be held accountable for the high failure rate.

Little did they know their fear and unwillingness to learn from the incident was costing the company more than $100,000 a month.

Paul was an extraordinary leader; he didn't give up. He wrote a memo to the company executives and informed them of the problem. Eventually, they investigated the situation and found Paul's observations true. Due to Paul's determination, they changed the policy to extend the furnace time and saved the company millions of dollars.

Extraordinary leaders aren't crippled by the burden of perfection. They're comfortable with making mistakes because they don't see it as a weakness. Instead, they view mistakes as ways to strengthen their leadership abilities and their organizations.

Innovation comes only with time, dedication and discipline. Until you get a grasp on it, your ideas may seem boring and useless. That's all right. Having less-than-great ideas or even ideas that others think are totally crazy is the stepping stone to success.

People thought Walt Disney's idea for making a movie starring a mouse with a falsetto voice was crazy. Back then, movies were still silent pictures. Producers couldn't imagine having voiced pictures, let alone one with a squeaky mouse. But Disney didn't give up.

Now millions of children worldwide have had the joy of laughing with and following the antics of Mickey Mouse. If Disney had not remained the innovative person he was, the world of animation may never have been launched and Disneyland, Disney World, Epcot Center and other theme parks may never have been built.

If you're willing to put forth the effort, innovation can be the road to your success as a leader. Begin today. Search your mind and everything around you for ideas. Then practice making them successful ventures.

Below I've provided a scenario to help you get started. Come up with the most inventive idea you can for solving the problem. I know it sounds like a boring issue, but that's the kind of situation ordinary people face—an ordinary problem. Your job is to solve it in an extraordinary way.

EMPOWERMENT WORKSHOP

You're leading the committee for setting the PTA's annual goals. The parents have been asked to fill out forms suggesting new goals.

Your job is to work with your team, compile the suggestions and offer a prioritized plan to the group president.

Two members of the team believe a school-wide project for raising money for the athletic department should head the list even though the only necessities at this point are new uniforms. They think it's a disgrace to have games in such an outdated gym.

Three others think the English enrichment program should be increased. They argue the purpose of education is to help students function in society, not play games in fancy buildings.

The other three believe the most important goal is improving parent-teacher relationships. They argue nothing will help the educational system more than facilitating cooperation.

How will you resolve this?

11

EMPOWERMENT PRINCIPLE #10
Leaders Maintain Perseverance and Tenacity

"Nothing in the world can take the place of persistence. Talent will not; nothing is more common than unsuccessful men with talent. Genius will not; unrewarded genius is almost a proverb. Education will not; the world is full of educated derelicts. Persistence and determination alone are omnipotent."

—Calvin Coolidge [67]

---

[67] George Sweeting, *Great Quotes & Illustrations* (Waco, Texas, Word Books, 1985), p. 201.

The Extraordinary Leader's Best-kept Secret

People said Colonel Sanders was too old. They said Albert Einstein was mentally retarded and Alexander Graham Bell was crazy. But what did they know?

Sanders, Einstein and Bell all knew the secret to their success—the key that made them extraordinary leaders. *They knew how to succeed in the face of incredible odds.* They had perseverance and tenacity.

American author Ambrose Bierce defined perseverance as "a lowly virtue whereby mediocrity achieves an inglorious success." [68] Perseverance *is* a lowly virtue. It's having the strength and willingness to go the lengths other people don't want to go. It's remaining steadfast when everything around you is on shaky ground. Mediocre people who persist despite opposition, discouragement and rejection will achieve inglorious success.

Colonel Sanders wasn't an outstanding person. He was an ordinary man who had what he thought was a great recipe. Because he had tenacity—stick-to-itiveness—he became a millionaire over some "finger-lickin' good" chicken.

Extraordinary leaders know the value of grooming perseverance and tenacity into their leadership approaches. They realize the only thing that gives them the edge is having more determination than the next person and pressing on no matter what.

---

[68] Ibid, p. 201.

> **Empowerment Principle #10:**
> *People who persevere and have strong tenacity know the
> secret to extraordinary leadership.*

The old saying goes, "Failure is the line of least persistence."
More persistence will produce success. Leaders who have
perseverance and tenacity succeed through trial and error; they
learn from their errors, reevaluate their options and resume
course at full speed.

Remember, it's all right to fail, but it's not acceptable to give
up. Philosopher Wang Yang-Ming once said, "The sages do not
consider that making no mistakes is a blessing. They believe,
rather, that the great virtue of man lies in his ability to correct
his mistakes and continually to make a new man of himself." [69]
Persevering is the test of true virtue.

The Rewards of Strong Will

In the 1940s a small, six-year-old Tennessee girl had
more than her share of troubles. Born prematurely, she
had contracted double pneumonia twice, developed scarlet
fever and had polio. As a result of the polio, she was
required to wear leg braces to correct her twisted left foot.
For six years she received rehabilitative treatment at a
nearby hospital. Every time she went for therapy, she
asked the doctor when she would be able to take off the
braces.

The young girl was determined to walk without those
braces. With the help of her brothers and sisters, for a
year she secretly took off the braces when her parents
were not home and painfully walked around the house to
strengthen her legs. Her persistence paid off. By the time

---

[69] Ibid, p. 186.

she turned 12 she could prove her accomplishment to the doctor, and he removed the braces.

But she didn't stop there. She had a vision of making a contribution in life and traveling the world. Nothing was going to get in her way. She set a goal to conquer any girl's sport she chose. That's when basketball came into the picture. Both she and her sister tried out for the team, but only her sister made it. However, her father made sure she was part of the team by telling the coach she had to be her sister's chaperon.

She sat on the bench that first season longing for her big break, but it never came. So she approached the coach and boldly stated she could become a world class athlete if he would give her 10 minutes of his time a day. He laughed, but he gave her the 10 minutes. While she tried to physically master his points, she soon realized her only instruction would be verbal, and it overwhelmed her. She couldn't seem to turn the instructions into basketball skills. She felt defeated.

With the help of two boys she had grown up with, she and her best girl friend started practicing every day. By the next season's try-outs they had both mastered the sport and made the team. During the season, the once polio-crippled girl became the team's second-best basketball player, right behind her best friend.

The team's regular referee, an internationally known track coach, was seeking girls who wanted to try out for a women's track team and he approached the number one and two basketball players. Trying her abilities in another sport, the young girl realized she could beat all her competition; *she* was finally number one.

When she started training seriously, her victories increased. One day her mentor, a two-time Olympic team member, asked her to try out for the Olympic track and field team. The 16-year-old qualified, but was eliminated in the semi-finals of the games. The defeat made her all the more determined to win the next time.

191

She continued practicing long, grueling hours, paid her way through college and maintained a B average. The next time she walked onto the field at the Olympic games there was no doubt in her mind she would stand on the middle platform and receive the gold for her country. She did—not just once, but *three* times.

Wilma Rudolph became the first woman in history to ever win three gold medals in track and field. To top it off, she ran the three races in record time. Wilma knew that in the face of all kinds of obstacles, determination breeds winners. [70]

The Way to Ensure Success

Extraordinary leaders make the effort and pay the price to ensure success. This determination goes along with the strong sense of commitment we talked about in Chapter 3. For extraordinary leaders, persistence doesn't have to result in gold medals, fame or money. The best results are making a difference, no matter how widely-known the leader or his or her efforts are.

A Missouri horse-breeder named Judy Piatt wasn't famous.[71] She was an ordinary person doing her job. Judy had a problem though; several of her horses had died in agony, and she could find no cause. Eventually she became convinced it had something to do with the oil sprayed on the stable floors to control dust.

It didn't matter that Judy lacked the technical knowledge to prove this. She was determined to find out what was in the oil that killed her horses. She started by following the trucks that delivered the oil. When she did, she discovered many headed back to dangerous chemical dump sites.

---

[70] Denis Waitley, *Seeds of Greatness* (Grand Rapids, Michigan: Baker Book House, 1983), pp. 189-197.
[71] Adapted from Earl Babbie, *You Can Make A Difference* (New York: St. Martin's Press, 1985), pp. 178-179.

She wrote state and federal officials about her discovery and listed the sites, but no one responded. Judy persevered. For 10 years she demanded that some kind of action be taken. Finally, the federal government looked into the incident. They discovered the oil was routinely mixed with a sludge rich in dioxin, a highly toxic compound.

As a result of Judy's persistence, the government uncovered and shut down dioxin sites throughout the country. Hundreds of thousands of people were probably spared an agonizing death from dioxin poisoning—all because of one extraordinary woman.

Judy was willing to make an effort even though she had no technical expertise with chemicals. She was willing to sacrifice 10 years of her time, energy and money to pursue an investigation. Now that's extraordinary leadership!

Determining Your Level of Persistence

Leaders need to establish their levels of persistence. In other words, just how much is the extra mile to you? If you're unwilling to go beyond the call of duty, you better think twice about becoming a leader. I haven't known a leader yet who wasn't required to sacrifice emotionally, physically and sometimes even financially. To do that you must be full of perseverance and tenacity.

Below is an empowerment exercise designed to help you discover where your level of persistence lies. Hopefully it's already at a high level, but if it's not don't lose heart. You can increase it.

EMPOWERMENT WORKSHOP

Honestly answer the following questions.

1. Do I always stick with a project until it's completely finished?

2. When I come up against a problem do I immediately begin searching for a solution?

3. Do I always view failures as learning experiences or growth opportunities?

4. When I'm caught in a situation where my expertise is not enough, do I come up with innovative ideas for seeking answers?

5. Do I concentrate on one goal at a time, or am I constantly trying to do several things at once?

6. Do I put 100% effort into everything I do?

7. Am I willing to work extra hours or weekends to accomplish a goal or finish an important project?

8. Do I press on toward my goal regardless of what other people say about me?

9. Do I view rejection as an opportunity to improve myself or my methods?

10. Do I maintain a positive attitude about things I try to do?

Ideally, you should have answered yes to all 10 questions. Few of us, however, can be that persistent all the time. It's hard to remain steadfast. It takes strong character and courage.

When I started playing the saxophone in elementary school, I got discouraged easily. My only lessons were in band classes, which didn't allow for much individual attention, and my progress seemed slow. However, I continued to practice, and I played well enough to join the high school band as a freshman. One day my first high school music teacher, Doris McCubbin, handed me a piece of music and said she wanted me to prepare this for the upcoming district music festival. She worked with me individually in preparing the solo, and I won a third rating. I set a goal to win a first rating and a chance to compete at the state level.

In my second year, Bob Schupp, my new music teacher, worked with me on my solo for the festival. That year I improved, with a second rating at the district contest. I still hadn't reached my goal. My junior year I won a first at district with a chance to enter the state festival. At the state festival I obtained a second rating, but now I had a new goal. I wanted to win a first in state competition. In my senior year I attained that goal.

The sense of accomplishment at winning a first rating in state competition and the joy I received from performing inspired me to set another goal: to go to college and major in music. I wanted to eventually teach music and conduct bands and orchestras. Again, after years of persistence and study, I achieved my goals. Perseverance and tenacity in my life has paid off.

Pressing on to the Goal

Effective leadership requires a courageous determination to press on until a vision becomes reality. I pressed on until I became a conductor. Wilma Rudolph pressed on until she won the gold. Lincoln keep running for offices until he became president, and Edison kept experimenting until he developed the incandescent light.

But how do you go about cultivating a high persistence level? I've found leaders can help foster the qualities of perseverance and tenacity in themselves by following 10 strategies:

1. Schedule and prioritize work.

In an earlier chapter we said the key to organization is prioritizing. The same is true for perseverance. It's much easier to stick to a project that's properly planned and strategized than one that's not. I've discovered if every night before I leave my office I write a list of priorities for the next day, I accomplish a lot more.

Priorities should be set in three categories:

Must Do Today

Should Do Today

Want To Do Today

By designating tasks into these areas, you avoid wasting time on low-priority projects that may be "want to do's" but don't necessarily have to get done.

EMPOWERMENT WORKSHOP

Choose one task you have to accomplish this week. Take time right now to prioritize your objectives to accomplish that task. Use the three categories and see if you can accurately schedule the time necessary to finish the project.

After a week, evaluate your progress. Could you have done something better? Could you have reorganized certain tasks?

2. Focus your sphere of influence.

Focusing is often one of the hardest things for leaders to do. Most people have several responsibilities and it can be difficult to focus on one at a time. To help you concentrate, determine what's most important to you right now.

Then decide which people, efforts, ideas and materials will benefit your goal most productively. If you come across something or someone that would benefit another project, make a note of it for future reference, but don't take time away from your current task.

Concentration takes great discipline and the ability to say "no." Don't be afraid to say no to people or other tasks that will hinder your concentration.

3. Be flexible.

Leaders need to be flexible. Things don't always go the way we want. Because of that, we need to be willing to make changes. If you thought your priorities were straight when you made them but now they don't seem to be working out, reorganize them. Changing your mind doesn't make you a poor leader; it proves your willingness to learn from ineffective decisions.

Don't allow yourself to become stagnant in a project or cause. If you're frustrated because nothing is getting accomplished, remember flexibility. There's no point wasting time remaining immobile. Take some chances; try a different angle.

4. Learn from mistakes and failures.

We've talked about this several times; for extraordinary leaders failing is not the end of the world. A wise person once said, "The glory is not in never failing, but in rising every time you fall." [72] If you fail, get up and try again. Edison failed 10,000 times before he invented the light.

---

[72]Earl Babbie, *You Can Make A Difference* (New York: St. Martin's Press, 1985), p. 109.

I'm not saying you should continue pursuing something even if it takes you 10,000 tries—that may be unrealistic. You could be doing something wrong. Remember these tips:

- If you fail at something two times, get some input from a person you trust. Try brainstorming out loud about why you failed and get his or her opinion on whether you should continue.

- If you fail again after you've done that, consider either trying a different approach or setting your vision to something a little more attainable.

5. Seek support.

Few people can persevere without the support of others. Most of the extraordinary people we've mentioned have had *someone* encouraging them and their ideas. Einstein had associates who were willing to work with him no matter how frustrated they got. Wilma Rudolph had a family and a mentor named Mae Faggs who believed in her and encouraged her to succeed.

If you're serious about cultivating a strong sense of perseverance and tenacity in your life, search out those people who can stand behind you regardless of the situation. They're the ones who will hold you up when you think you no longer have the strength to do so on your own. They're the ones who embrace your vision and inspire you to press on.

My wife has been this kind of supporter for me. Since my two children have grown, they, too, encourage me to succeed. Your supporters should be people willing to stand by you if you believe you're right, but they should also be people who offer constructive criticism to keep you on your toes.

Extraordinary leaders don't need people to always agree with them. They need people with similar goals who probe their minds and offer challenging suggestions.

198

```
EMPOWERMENT WORKSHOP
```

List three people or groups of people from whom
you could regularly seek support. In what ways do
you see them providing support? How can they
provide you the kind of assistance from which you
would benefit most? If you haven't already, ask
these people to be your support group.

6. Know when to refocus.

When we're really wrapped up in achieving a certain goal,
it's hard to admit things aren't working out. But changes are
necessary when our plans are consistently thwarted. Leaders
shouldn't be so proud they can't stop, review their plans and
possibly refocus them.

We need to take breaks when we're involved in difficult
situations, and leaders are no exception. It takes stamina to
remain dedicated to a cause the way Judy Piatt did. I'm sure
there were times during those 10 years she needed to take a
breather to see where she was going. She probably even
refocused her strategy several times to ensure the most
productive results.

7. Anticipate problems.

In the midst of perseverance Murphy's law will always
come into effect. What can go wrong will go wrong, so
prepare for it. Expect it, and don't act shocked when it
happens. One of the best ways to handle this is to have a
positive outlook. Extraordinary leaders need to convert what
appears to be stumbling blocks into building blocks.

199

Every problem has the potential to become a stepping-stone to your goal as long as you maintain the right perspective and look at it creatively.

EMPOWERMENT WORKSHOP

List three times when you could have turned a stumbling block into a building block but didn't. Specifically, how could you have used the situation to your advantage?

8. Specialize.

Specializing goes hand-in-hand with focusing on one project or task at a time. Leaders need to become specialists in one area before they try to move on to another. Concentrating your efforts on something you do well is less frustrating than constantly struggling over things you can't do well.

Be patient and take each task one step at a time. The time you spend gaining knowledge and expertise in one area will pay off in the long run.

9. Solve problems immediately.

When it comes to problem-solving, procrastination can kill your determination. Don't push problems out of the way because you can't handle them. They become harder to manage the longer they sit unsolved.

Leaders need to learn to take action. We all know the value of our time, and time means money. Leaders need to deal with problems immediately to save both time and money.

10. Commit to the long haul.

Perseverance and tenacity are both words that mean staying in for the long haul. If you're serious about any leadership role, make a firm commitment now. Do it before the going gets tough because it's a lot easier to give up then.

Recognize you may not see results immediately. It may take months, years or even a lifetime. Mozart's music wasn't recognized until after his death. But not seeing his goals become reality didn't discourage him. He pressed on.

Extraordinary leaders know success is not in the eyes of the world. It's in each person's soul. If you try your absolute best in everything you pursue, you will be a success, and that's all you can ask of yourself.

12

The Timeless Difference

"Perfection consists not in doing extraordinary things, but in doing ordinary things extraordinarily well."

—*Angelique Arnauld* [73]

"It is not titles that honor men, but men who honor titles."

—*Niccolo Machiavelli* [74]

---

[73] Eleanor Doan, *The New Speaker's Sourcebook* (Grand Rapids, Michigan: Zondervan Books, 1968), p. 41.

[74] As quoted by Sheila Murray Bethel, *Making A Difference* (New York: G.P. Putnam's Sons, 1990), p. 176.

Extraordinary Leaders Cast "Long Shadows"

Throughout this book, you've read about the leadership influence ordinary people can make in the world. An important point has been made repeatedly. Becoming an extraordinary leader is not something only the wealthy, prestigious or famous can achieve. Extraordinary leaders are people, like you and me, who leave lasting marks across the frontiers they plow. These leaders don't necessarily gain fame or fortune; rather, they make an impact, no matter how insignificant, that initiates a change in the world.

The Indians describe leaders with this kind of influence as people who cast "long shadows." Such leaders have made contributions to society extending beyond the immediate. Their contributions affect future generations in ways the leaders never imagined.

For example, Mother Teresa certainly never intended to become the internationally known leader she is. But her humble contributions to the destitute of India extend across continents and peoples of all kinds. She has truly cast a long shadow. Her extraordinary efforts not only earned her the Nobel Prize for Peace, but also assured her that generations to come would be informed of the pressing needs of the poor.

A Leadership Philosophy

Leaders who really wish to make a difference must live by a philosophy—not one of greatness, like many of us have been led to believe, but one of influence. Plenty of "great" people have hardly made what we'd consider far-reaching impacts in our world. On the other hand, several people have had an influence without attaining any measure of recognition.

When I envision those types of leaders, I think of all the teachers who guide our children, the concerned citizens who initiate community watch programs, or the parents who coach Little League teams or lead Girl Scout troops. Thousands of ordinary people do small things every day that really do leave lasting impacts.

A man I know in Erie, Pennsylvania, is casting a long shadow. He's Erie's consumer advocate when it comes to community utilities. He knows everything there is to know about utility rates.

Whenever a utility company proposes a rate increase, he pulls out his data and checks the latest information to see how the increase affects consumers. He involves the media to assure people are properly informed about fair rates.

This man doesn't hold any office or head any organization. He's just another ordinary person who works nine to five. But he doesn't want utility companies to take advantage of consumers, so he's placed himself in a leadership position to assure that members of the community are aware of the issues.

He informs people of the importance of taking a stand to support consumer rights and sets a precedence for more people to do the same in other areas. That makes him extraordinary.

This fellow, the Erie Advocate, isn't seeking media exposure for his own ego; he believes if he can influence just *one* person on the public utilities commission to see the consumer's side of the issue, he has made a difference.

The Fruit of a Vision

The most significant difference in people who remain mediocre and those who excel beyond the ordinary is: Extraordinary people turn their visions into reality. They establish goals, focus on them and stick to them until they see the fruit of their efforts.

That fruition doesn't happen overnight. A leader's influence is built over time. Influence is not a certain magnetism some people are born with and others aren't. It's a quality that can only be fine-tuned and polished when leaders are living examples.

How many times have you admired the leadership of another person only to find out he or she was living a lie? None of us is free from hypocrisy; it's a flaw of human nature. However, people who wish to become extraordinary leaders leave no room for others to doubt their sincerity.

Leaders make their impact through involvement, demonstration and loyalty. If you were helping an organization start a homeless shelter, you'd expect to see the leader of that mission exhibit "hands-on" involvement in the project.

That person would have to demonstrate a genuine attitude of service and prove his or her dedication to the homeless through *actions* not just words. Actions do more than make people think leaders are loyal to the visions, they prove loyalty.

Those Who Made a Difference

Extraordinary leadership can occur in all types of circumstances. Sometimes the extraordinary can happen when you least expect it. I'd like to share some stories about people who have proven their loyalty and leadership influence in unique situations.

Turning Grief into a Mission

Nancy Adams enjoyed spending time with her five-year-old daughter, Melissa. Adams didn't participate in any significant leadership roles other than motherhood and running a household. But one day in 1987, Melissa was abducted, sexually assaulted and murdered. Everything changed. This ordinary mother turned her grief and anger into an extraordinary mission

Adams started a program in her church to help educate parents about the importance of making their community a safer place for children. She eventually began to speak to other church groups and parent organizations in the schools. Determined to ensure that other parents and children not suffer as she and her family had, she accepted a leadership position in establishing a block-parent program in her neighborhood.

Eventually, through her efforts, other neighborhoods in the community created block-parent programs. She continues to speak regularly to church and school groups about child safety. Adams has made a lasting influence by doing something to achieve her mission. Because of her efforts, the people in her community are making it a safer place for all of their children.

Saving the Land

A twelve-year-old Pennsylvania boy became an environmental leader when he stopped construction of a small shopping mall on a ten-acre plot of land not far from his home.

James Marsdon would spend hours exploring this marshy area where he observed a variety of birds, small animals and water creatures. He even collected several samples of rare plants that he shared with his middle school science class.

To save the area and its wildlife, he consulted his science teacher for guidance, researched facts on the land and wrote letters to legislators and local officials. He collected signatures on petitions and eventually challenged the developers at a zoning hearing.

James' efforts came to the attention of a representative of the Department of Environmental Resources who suggested the area might be protected by law as a wetland. Through further research and the help of the DER representative, it was discovered that the area did, in fact, qualify as a bona fide wetland, and its destruction to accommodate a shopping mall would not be permitted.

A young boy who wasn't afraid to take the initiative demonstrated a dedicaiton far beyond his twelve years. He's an extraordinary leader casting a long shadow across the world of environmental conservation.

Making Beautiful Music

Mark Brackett, a barber and part-time professional musician from Chicago, moved to rural Missouri seeking a more leisurely lifestyle than that offered by the big city. In a town of 2,500 residents, he opened a one-chair barber shop on main street and immediately became active in the community.

Disappointed in learning the local school didn't offer instrumental music instruction, he persuaded school officials to allow him to offer class lessons in brass instruments two afternoons a week. There was a steady increase in the number of students wanting to study band instruments.

With help from the local parent-teachers group, Mark led a successful campaign to persuade the school board to hire a music teacher to develop a school band. The program flourished and he organized a band boosters club to help provide financial support.

Mark continued his interest in school and community music. Though his efforts, the city council enacted a band tax to support community music activities in the summer. With the cooperation of the school board, the music teacher was employed to develop a summer band comprised of interested school and community musicians. The summer band performed in area parades and presented weekly concerts in the city park.

The community recognized Mark Brackett for the long shadow he cast by building a bandstand in the park and naming it in his honor.

How You Can Make a Timeless Difference

It's clear we can't just follow an easy step-by-step strategy picked up from a book or swallow a vitamin to transform us from the ordinary to the extraordinary. Extraordinary leaders are not born, they're made. And the only way they're made is by honing skills and learning ways to establish lasting influence.

A leader's influence is the most valuable asset he or she has. We shouldn't miss the opportunity to cultivate a contributing level of influence.

I'd like to close this book with these five tips which have helped me learn to develop a lasting influence in any leadership capacity. I hope they provide some insight for you as well:

1. Always carry your compass.

Have direction and make sure others know what that direction is. You can't influence people or events without focusing on a clear, concise result.

2. Be the one to break ground.

Don't be afraid to step out into the unknown. Frontiers are the playing fields for extraordinary leaders. People will respect and want to follow leaders who are trail blazers. You will gain more influence by being a forerunner than by waiting for someone else to take the initiative.

3. Always give credit where it's due.

Leaders with lasting influence step away from the spotlight. They work hard to focus recognition on the performance of others. Influence comes from loyalty, and generosity breeds loyalty. A generous leader looks for the good things people do and compliments them for their efforts.

4. Promote enthusiasm.

When leaders are excited about what they're doing, they excite others and enlist them to their efforts. When organizations or groups are energized this way, incredible power lies behind their work.

5. Empower others.

If you're serious about casting a long shadow, the key is empowerment. I've based this book on 10 empowerment principles so you can become more resourceful as a leadership catalyst. The most important thing to remember is: Leaders only empower themselves to empower others. People may never notice how significant your influence was until after you're gone. If you want to become an extraordinary leader, then show someone else how to become one. A long shadow is a legacy worth pursuing.

RESOURCES

Dr. Don Panhorst

is currently a speaker, seminar leader and consultant who helps people enhance their leadership effectiveness and communication skills.

For further information about his programs, contact:

Dr. Don Panhorst
P.O. Box 725
Edinboro, PA   16412-0725
(814) 734-5814

Give the Gift of Leadership to Your Friends and Colleagues!

ORDER FORM

YES, I want _____ copies of *How Ordinary People Can Become Extraordinary Leaders* at $24.95 each, plus $3 shipping per book. (Pennsylvania residents please include $1.50 state sales tax per book.) Canadian orders must be accompanied by a postal money order in U.S. funds. Allow 30 days for delivery.

Name _____ Phone _____

Organization _____

Address _____

City _____

State _____ Zip _____

Please make your check payable and return to:

Baton Publishing Company
P.O. Box 725
Edinboro, PA 16412-0725

NOTES